Law and American Education

A Case Brief Approach
Second Edition

Robert H. Palestini
Karen F. Palestini

Rowman & Littlefield Education
Lanham, Maryland • Toronto • Oxford
2006

Published in the United States of America
by Rowman & Littlefield Education
A division of Rowman & Littlefield Publishers, Inc.
A wholly owned subsidiary of The Rowman & Littlefield Publishing Group, Inc.
4501 Forbes Boulevard, Suite 200, Lanham, Maryland 20706
www.rowmaneducation.com

PO Box 317
Oxford
OX2 9RU, UK

British Library Cataloguing in Publication Information Available

Library of Congress Cataloging-in-Publication Data

Palestini, Robert H.
   Law and American education : a case brief approach / Robert H. Palestini,
Karen F. Palestini. — 2nd ed.
      p.   cm.
   ISBN-10: 1-57886-394-5 (hardcover : alk. paper)
   ISBN-10: 1-57886-384-8 (pbk. : alk. paper)
   ISBN-13: 978-1-57886-394-5 (hardcover : alk. paper)
   ISBN-13: 978-1-57886-384-6 (pbk. : alk. paper)
   1. Educational law and legislation — United States — Cases. I. Palestini,
Karen F. II. Title.

   KF4118.P35 2006
   344.73'07—dc22
                                                              2005034765

∞™ The paper used in this publication meets the minimum requirements of
American National Standard for Information Sciences—Permanence of
Paper for Printed Library Materials, ANSI/NISO Z39.48-1992.
Manufactured in the United States of America.

Contents

Preface

Both public and nonpublic school educators are aware that courts, over the last several decades, have played an increasingly significant role in defining school policy. Decisions in such areas as school desegregation, prayer, public school financing, student rights, collective bargaining, students with disabilities, sexual harassment, and other personnel issues attest to the extent and importance of judicial influence. It is important, therefore, that teachers and administrators have at least a rudimentary knowledge and understanding of school law and how it affects their day-to-day classroom activities.

There is a sizable body of school law with which educators should be familiar if they wish to conduct themselves in a legally acceptable manner. Those educators who "fly by the seat of their pants" could have difficulty if sufficient thought is not given to the legal implications of their decisions and conduct. This text provides introductory material for those educators interested in K–12 educational issues, and who have little or no background or knowledge in school law.

Chapter One offers background regarding the sources of law and the structure of the judicial system that will enable readers to comprehend both procedurally and substantively significant aspects of cases and benefit from the information presented in succeeding chapters. Included in this chapter is a discussion of the legal significance of the sources of law, the federal and state constitutions and statutes, and the significance of the Fourteenth Amendment's due process and equal protection clauses. Also included is the organization of the American dual court system.

Chapter Two deals with the important issues endemic to nonpublic schools. It has been my experience that as many as one-third of the educators, especially in urban areas, are teaching and administrating in nonpublic schools. Oftentimes, the law affects these schools in a unique and different way vis-a-vis the public schools. This is particularly true for those schools that are religiously affiliated.

Chapter Three examines the extent of the state's and local school system's authority when individuals disagree with educational policy. This chapter explores the judiciary's attempt to establish a balance between the legitimate demands or objections of individuals toward education policy and school authorities' perception of their responsibility to the greater population. Such issues as compulsory school attendance, allowing religion in the schools, permitting the use of school facilities, providing aid to nonpublic schools, charging school fees, and providing health services are addressed.

Chapters Four and Five address issues pertaining to how the law affects students and teachers. Issues like freedom of expression, suspension, expulsion, corporal punishment, student searches, dress and grooming codes, pregnancy, parenthood, marriage, education of disabled students, and extracurricular activities. Teacher issues covered include non-renewal and dismissal, freedom of expression, academic freedom, drug testing, dress, employment discrimination, teacher collective bargaining, and political activities of teachers.

An historical legal perspective to the issues of school desegregation and legal attacks on the adequacy of state school finance formulae are the topics presented in Chapters Six and Seven. Although *Brown* was decided in 1954, the issue of school desegregation still haunts a surprising number of schools districts. Chapter Seven examines the issue of wealth disparity within a state as a factor in challenging a state's school financing plan. The issue emerged as a legal one in the early 1970s and continues to be a topical issue in many states. Also discussed in this chapter is the very controversial reform measure known as school choice.

This book takes a *case brief* approach to studying the law. Case briefs are the means by which students of the law summarize cases to facilitate learning and analysis. However, the examination of the full text of a case is invaluable. Thus, we encourage you to spend some time in a law library reading the full texts of appropriate landmark cases.

Finally, this book does not attempt to impose any particular view on the reader. Rather, the book's purpose is to provide those who are involved and interested in education with a rudimentary knowledge base for making educationally sound decisions within the legal framework of our nation. Having such knowledge could preclude, or at least minimize, an educator's exposure to liability. On the other hand, this book is not intended to scare educators into inaction. Many of the most effective learning activities carry with them a certain degree of risk. Field trips and laboratory experiments come immediately to mind. The knowledge obtained from this book is not intended to end the taking of field trips and the conducting of laboratory experiments. It is intended to be a guide to conducting these valuable activities in a responsible manner that will minimize the educator's exposure to liability.

Chapter One

Introduction

Under the American federal system, the three levels of government, federal, state, and local, all have a voice in educational matters, although not necessarily in unison or in equality. Although education is not specifically mentioned in the federal Constitution, the federal government has had a historic involvement in it. In fact, programs under various federal laws pertaining to education in recent years have made up approximately 6% of the total amount of money expended for public elementary and secondary education. Perhaps of greater importance has been the pervasive and significant force of the federal courts in influencing educational policy. Controversial education issues such as racial segregation in schools, financing of schools, due process for both students and teachers, the role of religion in the schools, and extent to which students and teachers may engage in freedom of expression have all been addressed by the federal judiciary.

State government has plenary power over public education, and this power is carried out by constitutional and statutory provisions, executive acts, state board of education policies, and actions of chief state school officers. Everything from the length of the school year to the qualifications teachers must have to educate their students emanate from state governments.

The degree of authority that local school systems have over educational matters depends on a state's constitutional and statutory provisions. These local powers may be delegated or implied. Although it is the prevailing belief that public schools are controlled locally, many students of educational governance suggest that, in fact, a so-called "myth" of local control exists. They argue that in many instances, especially when the state is heavily involved in financing education, the state has more meaningful power over education policy than the local school system does.

The difficulty of attempting to administer schools in a lawful manner is compounded when educators, unfamiliar with the nuances of the legal system, are confused by seeming inconsistencies and occasionally acrimonious disagreement among judges in certain court decisions. One remedy for ensuring lawful administrative conduct and reducing conflict and misunderstanding among educators is a systematic study of the sources of law under which educators operate. Although sources of law may be examined in various ways, a particularly useful method is to analyze those sources of law as they are issued by each level of government.

I. SOURCES OF LAW

A. Federal Law

1. Constitution and Amendments

Although the federal Constitution does not specifically mention education, its provisions have been used by litigants, and interpreted by the federal judiciary, to implicate educational issues. Particularly significant is the court's interpretation of the Fourteenth Amendment to the Constitution. The interpretation of the Fourteenth Amendment has been such a significant factor in educational legal theory that a further explanation of its impact is required.

Prior to the adoption of the Fourteenth Amendment in 1868, Americans had a kind of dual relationship with the state and federal governments regarding their civil rights that often resulted in the protection (or lack thereof) of one set of individual freedoms at the state level and protection (or lack thereof) of a completely different set of individual freedoms at the federal level. Historically, this came about largely as a result of a distrust of the central government that developed in revolutionary times as a consequence of experiences under British rule. To ensure that a central government would not again arbitrarily violate an individual's civil rights, a Bill of Rights, that is, the first ten Amendments, was added to the Constitution shortly after it was ratified. This Bill of Rights guaranteed Americans freedoms regarding religion, speech, press, peaceable assembly, etc. These protections, however, were those that Americans could only assert against the central government. They did not automatically have the rights to assert these freedoms against their state government as a result of their inclusion in the federal Constitution.

This dual relationship with state and federal governments and the historic primary allegiance to one's state was altered significantly by the adoption of the Fourteenth Amendment to the Constitution in 1868. This amendment provided, in part, that:

> All persons born or naturalized in the United States and subject to the jurisdiction thereof, are citizens of the United States and of the State wherein they reside. No State shall make or enforce any law which shall abridge the privileges or immunities of citizens of the United States. Nor shall any State deprive any person of life, liberty, or property, without due process of law, nor deny to any person within its jurisdiction the equal protection of the laws.

From a constitutional standpoint, the juxtaposition of the word "citizens" and "United States" is most revealing because, until this point in the history of the United States, Americans thought of themselves as citizens of their state first. Legally, then, this choice of words, as well as the primary reference to United States citizenship, sent a clear message that one's national citizenship was as important as one's State citizenship where the protection of individual rights was concerned.

This amendment, which was enacted shortly after the Civil War and intended initially to guarantee rights to ex-slaves, has provided individuals the right to freedom from arbitrary and capricious actions of state governments that might violate their civil rights. Effectively, the Fourteenth Amendment has served to make state governments accountable for actions they may undertake that unduly infringe or impede the individual freedoms articulated in the Bill of Rights (with certain, limited exceptions). Accordingly, since the passage of the Fourteenth Amendment, the rights individuals have as United States citizens cannot be unduly fettered by either the federal government or any state government, including local administrative actions or local school board policy.

In addition to establishing the primacy of national citizenship with the protection of certain individual rights, the Fourteenth Amendment also provides for due process and equal protection of the law. These two concepts stem from an ideal of fairness in applying the law, and are often used in conjunction in cases dealing with educational matters. Although extremely complex in a legal sense, these concepts may best be understood by keeping in mind that they require government actors, which often include educators, to be fair as they conduct governmental business.

Due Process. The *due process* clause of the Fourteenth Amendment serves two very different functions. First it imposes certain procedural requirements on governments before permitting them to infringe or deprive an individual's life, liberty or property interests. This concept is referred to as "procedural due process," and is implicated when a person is challenging the particular circumstances surrounding the government's taking of his or her individual life, liberty, or property.

Probably the most significant aspect of procedural due process is that it does not come into play unless and until a government takes a person's life, liberty, or property. In other works, there is no general requirement that governments provide fair procedures absent a taking of life, liberty, or property.

Although the concept of procedural due process will be raised in a number of cases presented in this book, the concept of "substantive due process" will have far greater application. For its part, substantive due process limits the states' substantive power to regulate certain areas of human conduct. In particular, states are prohibited from interfering with important individual rights that amount to an unreasonable (and unconstitutional) denial of liberty.

The determination as to what constitutes an important individual right for purposes of substantive due process is dependent upon whether the right in question is considered to be "fundamental" or "non-fundamental." Generally speaking, if the right in question is found in the Bill of Rights, it is considered a fundamental right.

A state or federal government cannot deprive an individual of a fundamental right without violating substantive due process (i.e., the Fourteenth Amendment) unless it can demonstrate that the governmental action was "necessary" to achieve a "compelling" governmental interest. This standard of review is called "strict scrutiny," and under this standard, government bears the burden of persuading the court that its actions were constitutional.

When a right is determined to be non-fundamental in nature, a different standard of review, called the "rational basis" test, is used. Under the rational basis test, the government's deprivation of the right in question will be constitutional if it is "rationally related" to a "legitimate governmental objective." Unlike the strict scrutiny standard of review, the plaintiff (that is, the individual who initiates the litigation), not the government, has the burden of persuading the court that the government is pursuing an illegitimate objective or that the means by which the government is pursuing a legitimate objective is not rationally related to that objective. A good example of the rational basis test can be demonstrated in a case where public schools decide to separate students according to their intellectual ability, as they often do in "tracking." Because the right to remain in the group of one's choice in school is not a fundamental right, the state's action (through its actor, the school district) of separating students will not be found to be unconstitutional unless the plaintiffs can show that the school district either used tracking to achieve an illegitimate objective (like separation of the races) or the means by which the school district pursued a legitimate objective (like ease of instruction) was not rationally related to that objective (if the tracking was done, for example, by a measurement of students' head circumference).

Equal Protection. From an educational standpoint, the Equal Protection Clause represents the legal basis for prohibiting unreasonable classifications. Although some type of classification is often necessary in laws, rules, or policies, arbitrariness may not play a part. Basically, the Equal Protection Clause guarantees that people who are similarly situated will be treated similarly, and that people who are not similarly situated will not be treated similarly. Methods of classifying students in schools have often been based on such factors as sex, age, intelligence, marital status, parents' residence, race, pregnancy or motherhood, conduct, test scores, and wealth of their community. For these methods of classification to conform with equal protection guarantees, they must reflect a meaningful educational difference between persons subject to the classification and persons not subject to the classification.

The Equal Protection Clause has been interpreted by the courts to impose a general restraint on the government's use of classifications to regulate human conduct or achieve governmental objectives. Presently, the courts recognize three levels of classification, which we will loosely refer to as: "suspect," "semi-suspect," and "non-suspect."

The classifications that are deemed "suspect" because they discriminate (or historically discriminated) against a politically powerless or unpopular minority include race and national origin. When a suspect classification is involved, the court subjects the government's action to the same strict scrutiny standard set forth in the preceding discussion concerning substantive due process (i.e., to be determined constitutional, the government must prove that use of the classification was necessary to achieve a compelling governmental interest).

"Semi-suspect" classifications include gender-based classifications, and are reviewed by courts using an "intermediate" scrutiny. Under the intermediate scrutiny standard, the government must demonstrate that the classification was "substantially related" to an "important" government interest. Almost every governmental interest advanced in support of a gender-based classification, with the exception of administrative convenience, has been determined to be "important" for purposes of the intermediate scrutiny test. However, a government's ability to demonstrate that its actions were "substantially related" to such an important interest has been far more difficult historically for a government to demonstrate.

Classifications made on bases other that those set forth in the preceding paragraphs are deemed "non-suspect." Non-suspect classifications, such as age, indigency, and mental retardation, are reviewed by the courts using the same rational basis test set forth in the preceding discussion concerning substantive due process and non-fundamental rights (i.e., to be deemed unconstitutional, the plaintiff must prove that the government's classification had no rational relation to a legitimate government objective—in other words, the classification was purely arbitrary).

Taking our example of the school district that classified students according to intellectual ability for tracking purposes, a court would start by asking what the basis for the classification is? In this instance, the basis for the classification is intellectual ability. Next, the court would determine whether the classification is suspect or semi-suspect. Since the classification does not involve race, linage, or gender, it is fairly safe to assume that the court would deem a non-suspect classification.

Once it is determined that a non-suspect classification is involved, the court will apply the appropriate test: the rational basis test. The court will then decide whether the classification has a rational relation to a legitimate government objective. In this case, the court will likely answer "yes" because there is legitimate government objective in ease of instruction to which the classification (based upon intellectual ability) is rationally related. Thus, this type of classification should be deemed constitutional.

2. Statutes

The Constitution (and the courts' interpretation of its provisions) is not the only standard by which the "justness" of any particular course of action is measured. Indeed, if this were the case, then any time a non-governmental actor misbehaved, it would go unredressed, and any time a person in a non-suspect class (such as the elderly, the indigent, and the mentally retarded) were discriminated against, they would have no means of obtaining relief.

Fortunately, this is not the case. Other sources of law require private persons to be responsible for their actions, and mandate fair (or at least fairer) treatment of certain classes of people (such as the elderly, the indigent, and the mentally retarded). Primary among these sources of law are statutes. Statutes are laws enacted by legislators at both the state and federal levels.

The United States Congress has enacted many statutes that provide educators and educational facilities with sources of law pursuant to which their actions must conform. The legal basis for this congressional involvement derives from the so-called General Welfare Clause of Article I of the United States Constitution. Some of the areas the national legislature has dealt with over the years include: vocational education (Vocational Education Act of 1963), defense (The National Defense Education Act of 1958), elementary and secondary education (Elementary and Secondary Education Act of 1965 commonly called Title I), civil rights (Civil Rights Act of 1964), protecting information concerning students (Family Educational Rights and Privacy Act of 1974, commonly called the Buckley Amendment), sex discrimination (Title IX of the Education Amendments of 1972), disabled children (Section 504 of the Rehabilitation Act of 1973, the Education for all Handicapped Children Act of 1975, and Individuals with Disabilities Education Act of 1990), bilingual education (Bilingual Education Act of 1968 and Title VII of the Elementary and Secondary Education Act of 1965), and pregnancy bias (Pregnancy Discrimination Act of 1978).

3. Regulations

Although the legislature, as our elected representatives, has the sole authority to enact legislation, the legislature may, and often does, delegate its authority to implement the statutes it enacts to executive agencies. Executive agencies routinely propose and adopt regulations to implement statutes.

Once agency regulations are adopted in accordance with proper administrative procedures, they are sources of law with the same power to regulate conduct as the legislation upon which they are based. Agencies often supplement these regulations with technical advice memoranda, advisory opinions, etc., which provide further insight into how the agencies believe certain statutes and regulations should be followed.

The regulations of many federal agencies affect education. For example, the Occupational Safety and Health Administration (OSHA) develops regulations that govern the safety of the educator's workplace, while the Environmental Protection Agency (EPA) oversees that the removal of asbestos in many school buildings is accomplished pursuant to certain environmentally acceptable standards. Although these regulations might not be specifically directed to education, they do regulate important respects of the educational environment.

4. Case Law

Basically, the federal courts are responsible for interpreting the various laws of the United States (and, in some cases, the individual states). The body of law that has been established by the courts is called case law. It is largely based on legal precedents declared in earlier court decisions in which there were similar factual situations. It is believed that following precedent affords a greater likelihood that litigants will be treated fairly, and it has the added advantage of allowing a degree of predictability in future disputes. Under the doctrine of *stare decisis*—which is Latin for "to abide by, or adhere to, decided cases," a court will prefer to stand by precedent and thereby not disturb a settled point of law. However, if the court judges that the factual situation in a particular case is sufficiently different from that of other cases, it is not bound by precedent. Furthermore, if following past precedent would result in a miscarriage of justice, the court may overrule a previous case, thereby establishing new precedent for the future. Courts are extremely loathe to do this, however.

The Federal courts have established a sizable body of case law that affects schools. Federal courts have addressed such issues as racial segregation, questions of equity of state methods of financing education, separation of church and state, due process and equal protection for both students and teachers, the extent of freedom of expression for students and teachers, and dress and grooming standards for students and teachers.

Although not always clearly understood and/or accepted by educators, a decision of the United States Supreme Court that interprets a federal law has the full force of law and may be altered or modified only by another Supreme Court decision or an Act of Congress amending the Constitution. Unfortunately, these kinds of United States Supreme Court decisions have not always been observed or followed by local school systems. In particular, desegregation decisions and those dealing with school prayer have been frequently ignored. Because the courts do not have an enforcement arm, the usual way people who are the victims of school systems' failures to observe United States Supreme Court decisions is to sue.

B. State Level

The major sources of law in this category are similar to those discussed in the federal category. They include the state's constitution, statutes, case law, state board of education policy, state department of education directives, rules and regulations of administrative agencies, executive order, and attorney general opinions.

1. State Constitutions

Almost every state constitution contains language committing the state to a responsibility for providing an education for its populace. Most often, the language will require the state to provide a thorough, efficient, and uniform system of education. Many states also have due process and/or equal protection of the law requirements similar to those found in the amendments to the federal Constitution.

2. State Statutes

State statutes represent a significant source of law that affect schools. They are often more explicit than state constitutional provisions, and their purpose is to bring a more specific outline of broad constitutional directives or to codify case law. Statutes may regulate governmental functions such as the method of selection, terms, and responsibilities of state-level education officials. They may also stipulate the type of local or regional school systems; the method of selection, responsibilities, and terms of local school officials; and the powers of local education units.

State statues also deal with financing of the public schools, tax instruments, and the degree to which these instruments may be employed to raise local revenue. Often teacher-pupil ratios are specified, as are the teaching of certain subjects, minimum and maximum ages for compulsory education, length of school day and year, and rules regarding suspension and expulsion of students. Other areas covered by state statutes include tenure, retirement, collective bargaining, and teacher dismissal procedures.

3. Case Law

There are notable exceptions, but in general, state courts historically have been reluctant to overturn existing school policies in the absence of clearly unreasonable, capricious, or arbitrary conduct on the part of school officials. Consequently, plaintiffs, when possible, have often opted to have their day in federal court instead of a state court. However, there still remains a large body of case law generated by the state court systems, especially in the area of common law, which will be discussed in further detail below.

4. State Board of Education, Chief State School Officer, and State Department of Education

The specific roles of the state board of education, the chief state school officer, and the state department of education vary considerably among the states; yet their offices collectively and individually provide an important source of law for educators.

Although the duties and responsibilities of state boards of education also vary, their primary function is to adopt the necessary policies, rules, and regulations to implement legislation and constitutional requirements. When not in conflict with constitutional decrees these policies, rules, and regulations have the force of law.

The chief state school officer, usually called the Secretary for Education, administers the state department of education, the agency that deals directly with the local school systems. The department is the bureaucratic mechanism through which state policy is transmitted to local systems.

5. Other Sources of Law

Sources of law with which educators in a local school system are most familiar are the local school board policies, rules, or regulations and their individual school's rules or regulations, usually contained in the school handbook. In many instances, building-level administrators rely on this authority in dealing with such issues as administering corporal punishment, suspending a student, searching a student, censorship of the school publications, student or teacher refusal to participate in patriotic exercises, use of a school building by members of the community, dress and grooming standards for both students and teacher, and the work rules emanating from the labor contract.

II. THE AMERICAN JUDICIAL SYSTEM

A dual judicial system composed of state and federal courts exists in the United States. Prior to instituting court action, with few exceptions, one must exhaust all local and state administrative remedies before seeking a redress of grievances through court litigation. Proceedings in school law often involve suits in which the facts are not in dispute, and the only question concerns purely legal issues (relating to due process and equal protection, for example). In this type of action, because there is no factual dispute, there is no jury, and judge is the sole determiner of how the legal question should be resolved, subject only to review by a higher court.

As part of his or her legal determination, the judge must consider present societal mores, actual or possible inconvenience or danger to society, precedent, and constitutional and other rights, where the balance lies between providing an individual with his or her constitutional rights and the legitimate demands of the larger society.

A. State Court Systems

Each state has the responsibility of establishing its own judicial system. Common to most states' judicial systems is a court of original jurisdiction and some sort of appeals structure.

In most instances, cases dealing with educational matters are initiated in the state's appropriate court of original jurisdiction. These courts are called circuit courts, district courts, courts of common pleas, or superior courts. Most litigation is settled in these courts, and they serve as the sole determiner of the facts, if they are at issue, in most cases.

Intermediate appellate courts constitute a second level of many state court systems. Where present, these appellate-level courts provide a tribunal between the trial court and the state's highest court of last resort. Their function is not to reevaluate the facts presented at the lower court level, but to determine whether the lower court correctly applied the law to the facts of the case before it.

Federal Court System

By constitutional design, the federal judiciary was established as a separate and independent branch of the United States government. Subsequent federal legislation has provided for a federal judicial system, which presently includes district courts, courts of appeals, and the United States Supreme Court. A litigant must raise a federal question (or meet the requirements of diversity jurisdiction) to have his or her case heard by a federal court. When dealing with educational issues, establishing federal question jurisdiction may be accomplished by alleging violation of a federal statute, or of amendments to the Constitution, such as the Fourteenth, First, Fifth, or Eighth

1. District Courts

The district court, of which there are over ninety, is the court of original jurisdiction for federal cases. Each state has at least one district court.

2. Courts of Appeals

Courts of appeals represent the intermediate appellate level of the federal court system. Their primary function is to review appeals from district courts within the circuit, and decisions by a court of appeals are binding on the lower federal courts. Courts of appeals base their decisions on the trial court's proceedings. A case may be remanded to a lower court for further proceedings when the appellate court finds that the facts presented are insufficient to render a decision.

3. Supreme Court

The court of last resort in the United States is the Supreme Court. There is no appeal from a decision rendered by this Court. Nine justices, including the chief justice, make up the Court. As with all federal judges, their appointment is for life.

Most cases reach the Supreme Court by means of a *writ of certiorari*. Under this method, an unsuccessful litigant in a lower court decision petitions the Court to review the case, setting forth reasons why the case should be heard. Four judges must vote to hear the case in order for certiorari to be granted.

The Supreme Court's term begins on the first Monday in October and lasts nine months. Although the Court decides between 200 and 250 cases in a term, formal written opinions are rendered in approximately half of these cases.

Although the right of judicial review is not explicitly provided for in the United States Constitution, many scholars agree that the framers of the Constitution expected the Supreme Court to assume this function. The Court's role as the final authority in interpreting the Constitution through judicial review was established in its landmark decision, *Marbury v. Madison*.

Chapter Two

The Educator and Liability

Educators are often primarily concerned with how the law affects them on an individual basis. They wonder about the extent to which they will be held personally accountable for their role in depriving someone of his or her constitutional rights, administering corporal punishment, failing to supervise students properly, and general acts of malpractice.

The area of law that addresses these concerns is known as *tort law*, which is defined as a civil wrong in which one suffers loss as a result of the improper conduct of another. Although improper conduct can be intentional, reckless, and/or negligent, most of the tort law referenced in this book focuses on negligence.

The question that often arises from nonpublic schoolteachers and administrators is how these schools differ from public schools in how the law affects them. It is appropriate to make that distinction here. In a nutshell, because nonpublic schools are not considered state governments (or agents of state governments), their actions are not restricted by the Constitution. However because nonpublic schools are persons—the term person is used broadly in the law to refer to both natural persons and corporate or institutional entities—they are deemed to have the duty to observe certain standards of conduct imposed upon all persons in a given community. For this reason, nonpublic schools are subject to tort and contract law but not subject to constitutional law. Because public schools are both agents of the state governments and legal persons, they are subject to both constitutional law and tort and contract law.

Despite the fact that nonpublic schools are not required to protect the rights articulated in the Constitution, most of these schools voluntarily provide these rights to some extent to their students and especially to their teachers. Religiously affiliated schools may be exempted from providing constitutionally protected freedoms because they are considered "churches," separate from the state and state government by virtue of the First Amendment, and therefore, are not considered governments or agents of the government. Likewise, nonsectarian nonpublic schools are usually exempted from adhering to constitutional law because they do not receive significant enough revenue from the government to be considered agents of the government. They, too, usually voluntarily provide students and teachers with constitutional rights.

As stated, all schools and the educators who work in them are responsible for observing the protocols of tort and contract law. This means that, for schools having a student handbook, they must adhere to the terms of the handbook as a "contract" between the school and the students and their parents. In addition, the schools must perform in accordance with the standards of care prevailing in their communities—in most cases, this means at a minimum, they must provide a "safe place" and "reasonable supervision" to students placed in their care.

I. SCHOOL DISTRICT IMMUNITY

A. Liability under State Law

In about half the states in the nation, public school districts have sovereign immunity from liability for torts committed by the school districts and their employees. This position is based on the old adage that "the king can do no wrong." Therefore, the government, in this case school districts, cannot be sued without their consent. Many legal scholars have been critical of the doctrine of sovereign immunity because it often leaves an injured party without any meaningful compensation for losses.

Historically, the immunity of school districts did not protect individual school employees from liability in tort. Many states, however, have reconsidered this notion, arguing that the individual school employees are least able to defend themselves in court. In Georgia, for instance, immunity has been extended to school principals and to classroom teachers. See *Hennessy v. Webb,* 264 S.E.2d 878 (1980), and *Truelove v. Wilson, 285* S.E.2d 556 (Ga. 1981).

B. Liability under Federal Law

As you might have inferred from our earlier discussion of sources of law, simply because a suit against a school district may be prohibited under *state* law, it does not necessarily follow that the same suit against the school district or the individual officers or employees of that school district, cannot be brought under *federal* law. Although admittedly complex, a short explanation of state sovereign immunity and federal power should prove beneficial to your understanding of the following cases involving the recovery of monetary damages for alleged civil violations by school districts and school officials/employees.

1. The Eleventh Amendment

Pursuant to the Eleventh Amendment of the United States Constitution, "(T)he judicial power of the United States shall not be construed to extend to any suit . . . commenced . . . against one of the United States by Citizens of another State, or by Citizens or subjects of any Foreign State." Although the text of the Eleventh Amendment would appear to allow in-state citizens to sue their own state of citizenship, the Supreme Court has interpreted the eleventh Amendment to bar in-state citizens as well as out-of-state citizens from suing a State. *Hans v. Louisiana* 134 U.S. 1 (1890); *Pennsylvania v. Union Gas Co.*, 491 U.S. 1 (1989).

Today, the Eleventh Amendment serves as a venue for any private citizen attempting to sue a state, subject to certain important exceptions. Among these exceptions are:

• Suits against state *officers*—a federal court may enjoin (prohibit) a state official from violating federal law. The legal fiction underlying this exception is that a suit against a state *officer* is *not* a suit against the *state.*
• Suits in which the state consents—a state may waive the protection of the Eleventh Amendment by consenting to suit, whether by voluntarily appearing in federal court to defend itself or by passing a statute that allows itself to be sued.
• Suits arising under the Constitution and suits arising under laws passed pursuant to Congress' power under the Constitution to abrogate (abolish) state sovereign immunity.
• The states are not immune from suits arising under the Constitution.
• Congress may abrogate state sovereign immunity through statutes that are passed pursuant to the Fourteenth Amendment (i.e., Civil Rights legislation) so long as Congress *clearly states its intent to abrogate* state sovereign immunity. As we will see in cases briefed further along in this chapter, the courts have found no clear intent to abrogate under the basis Civil Rights Act 42 U.S.C. section 1983 (dealing with deprivation of Constitutional rights under color of state law), while the courts have found a clear statement of intent to abrogate under Title VII of the Civil Rights Act of 1964 (dealing with discrimination in the places of public accommodation).
• Suits brought against subdivisions of the state—the Eleventh Amendment does not bar suits brought against counties, municipalities, and school boards by citizens of the state.

2. Congressional Power to Enforce Constitutional Rights

As you now know, the Fourteenth Amendment restricts certain actions of the states themselves, as well as certain actions of private agents who act on behalf of the states. Pursuant to the Necessary and Proper Cause of Article I,

Section 8 of the Constitution—providing that Congress may "make all laws which shall be necessary and proper for carrying into execution . . . all powers vested by the Constitution in the government of the United States . . ." and pursuant to the Enabling Clause of the Fourteenth Amendment—which empowers Congress to enforce the Amendment by "appropriate legislation"—Congress is authorized to pass legislation extending the protections granted under the Fourteenth Amendment and holding private persons accountable for violations of the same. Accordingly, Congress may impose criminal or civil remedies upon anyone who interferes with someone's constitutional rights; (1) when "acting under color of law" (see the text of 42 U.S.C. 1983, below)—when state or local officials misuse the authority of their positions to violate an individual's Fourteenth Amendment rights; and (2) when acting in his or her private capacity. Thus, Congress has the power to pass laws protecting constitutional freedoms from being deprived by *anyone*.

3. Liability under 42 U.S.C. 1983

A section of the Civil Rights Act of 1871 provides for liability if a person operating under the color of the state violates another person's rights. Specifically, the law states:

> *Every person who, under the color of any statute, ordinance, regulation, custom, or usage, of any State or Territory or the District of Columbia, subjects, or causes to be subjected, any citizen of the United States or other person within the jurisdiction thereof to the deprivation of any rights, privileges, or immunities secured by the Constitution and laws, shall be liable to the party injured in an action at law, suit in equity, or other proper proceeding for redress . . . 42 U.S.C. 1983.*

Although this law had not received much judicial attention for nearly a hundred years, several recent Supreme Court decisions have addressed school district and school officials' liability and the extent, if any, of damages under it. **Wood v. Strickland** addresses the issue of school board member immunity for liability under Section 1983, while **Carey v. Piphus** clarifies the elements and prerequisites for recover of damages under this act.

Wood v. Strickland
420 U.S. 921, 95 S. Ct. 1589, 43 L. Ed. 2d 214 (1975)

Topic: Exception to sovereign immunity; state liability under Federal Law.

Facts: Peggy Strickland and Virginia Craig, 10th graders at Mena Public High School in Arkansas, were expelled from school for violating a school regulation prohibiting the use or possession of alcoholic beverages at school or at a school activity.

Issue: Whether the student's federal constitutional rights to due process were violated by their expulsions and, if so, whether the school board is immune from liability under Civil Rights Act of 1871 (42 U.S.C. § 1983).

Holding: Public high school students do have substantive and procedural rights while at school. *See Wood*, 420 U.S. at 326. In the specific context of school discipline, a school board member is not immune from liability for damages under §1983 if he knew or reasonably should have known that the action he took was within his official responsibility. *See Id.* at 322.

Reasoning:

Major Premise: A state enjoys immunity from liability for its actions, but it may not violate an individual's right protected under the United States Constitution.

Minor Premise: Exception to sovereign immunity; state liability under Federal Law. Public school students have rights protected by the United States Constitution.

Conclusion: When a state violates the Constitutional rights of public school students, the state is liable under the Civil Rights Statute codified as 42 U.S.C. § 1983.

Carey v. Piphus
435 U.S. 247, 98 S. Ct. 1042, 55 L. Ed. 2d 252 (1978)

Topic: Recovery of damages under the Civil Rights Act of 1871 as codified in 42 U.S.C. § 1983.

Facts: Two public school students were suspended without being given an adjudicatory hearing. The students claimed that they were suspended in violation of the Fourteenth Amendment's procedural due process requirement.

Issue: Whether the Fourteenth Amendment of the United States Constitution permits students to recover damages when they are suspended from public elementary and secondary schools without procedural due process, in the absence of proof of injury.

Holding: Yes, the right to procedural due process is "absolute" in the sense that it does not depend upon proof of actual injury. *Carey*, 435 U.S. at 266. Therefore, the students can still recover nominal damages, in this case, one dollar. *See Id.* at 267.

Reasoning:

Major Premise: The procedural safeguards of the Fourteenth Amendment are invoked when a significant constitutional right is at stake, regardless of the outcome of the underlying dispute.

Minor Premise: Procedural due process rights must be scrupulously observed, and this is viewed distinctly and separately from violations of substantive rights, which are compensated upon showing of actual injury.

Conclusion: School officials are liable for procedural due process right violations even if the students could not prove actual injury.

2. Damages under Title IX

A unanimous ruling by the Supreme Court in **Franklin v. Gwinnett County Schools** upheld a claim for monetary damages under Title IX when intentional sexual harassment was shown. This decision provides victims of sexual discrimination with a potent legal remedy.

Franklin v. Gwinnett Cy. Pub. Schools

503 U.S. 60, 112 S. Ct. 1028, 117 L. Ed. 2d 208 (1992)

Topic: Damages remedy under Title IX of the Education Amendments of 1972 prohibiting sex discrimination.

Facts: A high school student was subjected to continual sexual harassment and abuse, including coercive intercourse, by a male teacher at the school operated by the Gwinnett County school district in Georgia. She sued under Title IX claiming that the school was aware of and investigated the matter, but took no action to stop it and discouraged her from pressing charges. The District Court dismissed the student's complaint on the grounds that Title IX did not authorize an award of damages. The United States Court of Appeals affirmed.

Issue: Whether the implied right of action under Title IX supports a claim for monetary awards.

Holding: Yes, the United States Supreme Court reversed. The Court held that a money damages remedy is available for an action brought to enforce Title IX.

Reasoning:

Major Premise: If there is a traditional presumption in favor of the availability of an appropriate relief, even if Congress is silent on the question of remedies, a federal court has the power to award the appropriate relief. *See Franklin*, 503 U.S. at 66.

Minor Premise: An implied right of action exists under Title IX. *See Cannon v. University of Chicago*, 441 U.S. 677 (1979). The Court presumes the availability of all appropriate remedies unless Congress has expressly indicated otherwise. *See* 503 U.S. at 66.

Conclusion: An award for money damages is available for an action brought under Title IX prohibiting sex discrimination.

II. THE LAW AND NONPUBLIC SCHOOLS

Because, in many parts of the nation, it is common for a full one-third of the teachers and administrators in a given geographic area to be employed in nonpublic schools, it is important to note the legal idiosyncrasies that apply to these schools. As you might suspect, because these schools are not "state actors" for purposes of the Fourteenth Amendment—see separation of church and state discussion, below—actions that these schools (or their agents) undertake that have the purpose or effect of denying a liberty interest articulated in the Constitution are not prohibited by the Constitution. Why is a nonpublic school not a state actor in the same sense as public school, and, therefore not subject to the constraints imposed by the Fourteenth Amendment? The answer is that nonpublic schools are considered "religions," with regard to which the state must remain separate.

A. Special Status of Religious Schools

The "religion clauses" of the First Amendment provide:

Congress shall make no law respecting an establishment of religion, or prohibiting the free exercise thereof.

The first, "establishment," clause of this Amendment goes beyond forbidding a state church, but it does not prohibit every action of a governmental body that results in a benefit to religion. The overriding goal is a "benevolent neutrality" by government as it concerns religion. See *Walz v. Tax Commission*, 397 U.S. 664 (1970).

Generally speaking, the Establishment Clause prohibits government sponsorship of religion, government funding of religion, and active participation in religions' activities. Therefore, the states' involvement in certain aspects of religiously affiliated nonpublic school activities is unconstitutional. The specific test used by the courts to determine constitutionality of state involvement (through transportation, textbooks, health services, tuition grants, and tax credits) in religiously affiliated schools is set forth in the next section as the **Lemon** test.

Because many private schools (both religiously affiliated and non-religiously affiliated) receive no state or federal aid, government can only regulate in a very limited area. As you might imagine, even though Congress has the power under the Necessary and Proper Clause to pass laws extending to private persons, including nonpublic schools, many rights and protections afforded under the Fourteenth Amendment, there are still some areas relating to personal liberties that have not been so extended by Congressional intervention. However many of these areas are the subject of state and local public health and welfare, such as fire codes and child abuse statutes, as well as private contract law and state common law.

Accordingly, even though free speech, due process, and equal protection rights may not be imposed upon non-public schools by the Constitution or by Congressional action under the Necessary and Proper clause, contract law and state common law, which are generally applicable to both public and nonpublic schools, will define the scope of right to be afforded to students, parents, and teachers in the nonpublic school setting. Prudence, however, suggests that students, parents, and teachers be afforded their constitutional rights, even in nonpublic schools.

B. Duties of Nonpublic Schools as Private Citizens

As private citizens, schools have the duty to conduct themselves in accordance with the civil law respecting contractual undertakings and negligence law. We will explore the schools' requirements regarding negligence law later in this chapter. But because contract law is often the source of the relative rights afforded students, parents, and teachers in nonpublic schools, we will focus on that issue here.

As a general rule, contract law regulates relationships between both the public and the nonpublic school and its students. However, because nonpublic schools charge tuition, they are most vulnerable to judicial interference with their right to administer the school on theories of breach of contract.

The nonpublic school offers an education that the student accepts by the payment of tuition, thus constituting a contract. The terms and conditions of the contract are usually set forth in the student handbook. Therefore, the handbook is vital in disputes involving breach of contract. Courts normally uphold the school if it can be shown that the expectations for student behavior are duly promulgated in the handbook. Thus, the value of a clearly worded and legally accurate student handbook cannot be overestimated.

III. EDUCATOR LIABILITY

A tort is, quite simply, a civil wrong. In most states, tort law has evolved through a series of state case law decisions, often referred to as *common law*. There are many torts that affect educational relationship. Depending upon the mindset of the alleged perpetrator, the tort is deemed "intentional," "reckless/grossly negligent," or "negligent."

A. Intentional Torts

Intentional tort law applies to both public and nonpublic schools. As the name suggests, these kinds of torts require intent to commit the act by the alleged wrongdoer. The most common intentional torts with which educators become involved are assault and battery. Battery is the unpermitted and unprivileged contact with another's person, such as striking someone. Physical and/or emotional damages are not required to bring suit. Assault is the placing of someone in apprehension of immediate harmful or offensive contact. "Offering someone out" to settle an issue is another example of assault. Obviously, threatening someone with a weapon, which unfortunately, seems to be occurring more often in schools, is a more extreme example of assault.

Although the courts have demonstrated wide latitude in their treatment of these types of cases, a teacher may be charged with assault and battery as a result of disciplining a student. In many states, assault and battery carry criminal as well as civil penalties with them, depending upon whether the government (prosecutor's office) and/or the alleged victim brings suit. It should be noted that, although the tort of assault and battery may involve a significant monetary judgment, the crime of assault and battery can carry both monetary penalties and jail sentences with it. In civil assault and battery suits, a teacher could be held liable if he or she administered corporal punishment of any kind or degree, whether while angry or in a brutal, cruel, or excessive manner. Other factors taken into consideration to determine the extent of the teacher's potential monetary exposure would be the location on the body where the child was struck, the child's age, the child's mental capacity, and the nature of the offense. We will see (*Ingraham v. Wright*) that from a constitutional standpoint, a teacher is not prohibited from administering reasonable corporal punishment, but it is not always prudent to do so because of liability imposed under intentional tort law. Also, many school districts have a local prohibition on corporal punishment.

B. Defamation of Character

Defamation of character torts can take two forms, libel and slander. Libel is placing unsubstantiated derogatory comments about someone in writing. Slander is saying something derogatory about an individual without being able to substantiate it. These types of charges are increasingly being made against teachers. Teachers who voice their opinions of students in public need to be circumspect with regard to their comments. Because many of these suits contend that psychological and emotional damage was caused by the derogatory comment, the teacher becomes very vulnerable. It is very difficult to anticipate the psychological impression that such comments will have on each individual. The best defense is not to make such comments.

Placing such comments in writing can be even more problematic. Making comments on test papers and on permanent record cards is a common practice of teachers. However, care should be taken that such remarks are not slanderous. Now that the Family Educational Rights and Privacy Act of 1974—P.L. 93-380 (Buckley Amendment) permits students and parents "the right to inspect and review any and all official records, files, and data directly related to their children, including all material that is incorporated into each student's cumulative record folder," teachers should be even more careful about the terms that they use in describing and assessing a student.

C. Negligence

Negligence law is another area of jurisprudence that affects both public and nonpublic schools. An educator may be liable if an injury to a student results from the educator's negligence. Liability for negligence may occur if it can be shown that the alleged negligent party should have anticipated the possible harmful results of his or her actions or inactions. A commonly employed test to determine negligence is whether a reasonable and prudent degree of care has been exercised.

Several elements must be present to have a valid cause of action for negligence: (1) a legal duty to conform to a standard of conduct generally recognized as necessary and appropriate for the protection of others, (2) a failure to exercise, or "breach" of, this standard of care, (3) a causal connection often referred to as "proximate cause" between the conduct and the resultant injury, and (4) actual loss or damage as a result of the injury.

1. Duty of Care

The common laws of most states have established a teacher–student relationship that imposes a duty of care on the part of teacher. In some states, statutory provisions reduce the amount of liability that teachers have to their students within the educational environment, and only impose liability for willful or wanton misconduct.

2. Standard of Care

For the most part, the standard of care a teacher must exercise to avoid liability is defined as that of the "reasonable and prudent" person. The standard of care varies according to such factors as the age of the student, the child's mental capacity, and environment and circumstances under which an injury took place. The amount of care due school children increases with the immaturity of the child; therefore, it is expected that greater care will be given while supervising extremely young children.

A higher degree of care should be exercised in such potentially dangerous situations as chemistry laboratories or shop classes. A teacher is not necessarily liable for all injuries sustained by students, but whenever an injury occurs, the question of whether it should have been foreseen and what steps were taken to avoid potential injury will be raised.

3. Proximate Cause

In order for liability to be established, a causal connection must exist between a teacher's conduct and the injury incurred. The teacher's negligence must be a substantial cause of the injury to the student. However, if the cause of the injury can be shown to be the result of an intervening act or the responsibility can be legitimately shifted to another person, the liability may be mitigated. For example, if there are holes in the macadam of the schoolyard, and an injury takes place as a result, the liability may be shifted from the teacher to the school district, which has responsibility for maintaining the schoolyard.

4. Actual Loss or Injury

Actual damage has to be demonstrated in order for negligence to be found. In these cases, psychological or emotional damage must manifest itself in some demonstrable way. If physical damage is alleged, it must also be proven.

D. Defenses for Negligence

Some common defenses for negligence are contributory negligence and assumption of risk. Contributory negligence may be available as a defense if it can be demonstrated that the injured party failed to exercise the required degree of care necessary to ensure his or her own safety. However, this defense is not always available to teachers of young children in that the courts usually perceive children as not being able to care for themselves.

Assumption of risk may also be available as a defense when the injured party could or should have anticipated the potential risk involved in participating in a more inherently dangerous type of activity. For example, the rugby team members should anticipate that the risk of injury is significantly greater than it is for members of the school newspaper staff. So, if the coach of the rugby team is cited for negligence in the case of an injury fairly common among rugby players, the coach is likely to be able to use assumption of risk as a defense.

IV. DUTIES OF SUPERVISION

The following brief descriptions of court decisions are offered as illustration, although caution should be exercised in generalizing from them because the details of a particular case might vary enough from these examples, depending upon the state in which the educational process is taking place, as to make them inapplicable.

A. Before and after School

Unless the students are on school buses, the courts generally do not find a duty on the part of schools and teachers to supervise students on their way to and from school. For example, in a case where a seven-year-old child was killed while crossing a road in front of his school, a Louisiana appellate court, in *Johnson v. Ouachita Parish Policy Jury*, 377 So.2d 397 (La. Ct. App. 1979), held that the public school did not have a legal duty to provide safety patrols or adult school crossing guards.

Once the students are on school property before or after school, however, the burden of responsibility becomes greater. For example, adequate supervision must be afforded students for a reasonable time as they congregate and wait for school to begin in the morning. In a New Jersey decision, *Titus v. Lindberg,* 49 N.J. 66, 228 A.2d 65 (1967), a principal was held liable for an injury that happened to a student before school. In this instance, the injury resulted from a paper clip that was propelled by a student waiting for transportation to another school. It was customary for students to arrive at school about 8:00 am, although the classrooms did not officially open until 8:15 am. This incident occurred at approximately 8:05 am. The court offered several reasons for its holding that the principal's negligent supervision was the proximate cause of the injury: his failure to announce rules concerning playground supervision before school, to assign teachers to supervision, and personally to provide adequate supervision.

Similar findings have occurred with regard to after-school activities, especially sports activities. In Pennsylvania, a student was killed by another student in a javelin accident. Both students were members of the track team, and the incident occurred in the locker room after practice, while the coach remained on the track to give individual instruction to other team members. Although the case was settled out of court, the belief was that the courts would have found the coach and the school district liable for lack of reasonable supervision and negligence.

B. During School Hours

During school hours the requirements of reasonable and prudent teacher supervision are expected. Schools must not only provide supervision in the classrooms, but also during recess, in the halls, or during the lunch hours. The California Supreme Court, in *Dailey v. Los Angeles Unified School District,* 470 P.2d 360 (Cal. 1970), contended that school authorities were negligent in the supervision provided at a noon recess. In this case, two high school students engaged in a fight that resulted in the death of one of the students. The court contended the school was negligent not to have a comprehensive schedule of supervision assignments and proper instructions for subordinates as to what was expected of them while they were supervising.

A physical education teacher was found to have a duty of properly instructing students before a vertical jumping exercise was attempted. After she failed to provide sufficient instruction, a child suffered injury when she ran into a wall while performing the exercise. See *Dibortole v. Metropolitan School District of Washington Township,* 440 N.E.2d 506 (Ind. Ct. App. 1982).

C. Off-Campus Activities

Participation in off-campus activities, such as a field trip, or interscholastic activities, such as athletics or debate, places the school in the same position of duty to use care to prevent injury as if the students were on campus.

A school district was found negligent in failing to provide adequate supervision at a downtown showing of a controversial movie entitled *King,* at which event students' attendance was required. Students were bused to the theater accompanied by chaperones. Obscene racial comments were made by both Caucasian and African-American students during the showing. Upon leaving the balcony for the lobby, a student was pushed, her wrist slashed, and her purse taken. The Minnesota Supreme Court in *Raleigh v. Independent School District No. 625,* 275 N.W.2d 572 (Minn. 1979), upheld the awarding of damages against the school for failure to provide sufficient precautions in the light of having knowledge about racial tensions.

V. PARENTAL CONSENT

It is preferred that parents give written consent for participation in extracurricular activities and field trips because it demonstrates that the school is attempting to provide reasonable supervision and a "safe place" for the students. However, one should never presume that written permission will preclude a legal suit. Although a parent may waive his or her right to sue on behalf of a student child, the child's right to sue often survives as an independent right.

This issue was addressed by the Washington Supreme Court, which held invalid, as against public policy, the practice of requiring students and their parents to sign a release of all potential future claims as a condition to student participation in certain school-related activities, such as interscholastic athletics. See *Wagenblast v. Odessa School District No. 105-157-166j*, 758 P. 2d 968 (Wash. 1988).

VI. CONTRACT LAW

Another area of law that affects both public and nonpublic school alike is contract law. Contract law may affect nonpublic schools even more than public schools because nonpublic school parents pay tuition directly to the school. Because they pay for the educational services directly, rather than through tax dollars, nonpublic school parents tend to view the relationship with the school as being a contractual one more often than do public school parents.

As a general rule, contract law regulates relationships between both the public and nonpublic school and its students. The school offers an education, which the student accepts by payment of tuition or taxes. The "terms and conditions" of the contract are set forth in the student handbook and the policies and procedures of the school and the school system. Obviously, the student handbook is vital in breach of contract disputes with students and their parents. Courts will ordinarily uphold the school if it can be shown that the expectations for student behavior are duly promulgated in the student handbook. Thus, it is important that this document be scrutinized to be certain that the "conditions" of the contract are clear and reasonable.

Ambiguous language in the student handbook can be problematic. For example, there was a parochial school that was interested in having its students reflect the values that they were taught even when they were off school property. Thus, the school had a statement in its school handbook that read, "Students and School X are expected to act like good Catholic ladies and gentlemen, even when off school property." It so happened that a group of students rented a school bus in the school's name to transport them to an amusement park on a school holiday. On the way to the park, students began using abusive language and making obscene gestures to passing motorists. One of the motorists used his car telephone to alert the police of the incident. The bus was pulled over and the students' conduct was reported to the school. The school suspended the students on the grounds that their behavior was unbecoming that of a "good Catholic." However, the suspension had to be lifted when several on the parents of non-Catholic students pointed out that this particular "condition" of the "contract" that they had with the school did not apply to them. In order to treat everyone equally, then, the school decided that it could not discipline anyone. The obvious lesson to be learned is the importance of clear and unambiguous language in the student handbook.

VII. SEXUAL HARASSMENT

In the last decade, the instances of sexual harassment have escalated. Sexual harassment is a form of sexual discrimination and is in violation of Title VII and Title IX of the Civil Rights Act of 1964. Sexual harassment is defined as verbal or physical conduct of sexual nature, imposed on the basis of sex, by an employee or agent of a recipient that denies, limits, provides different, or conditions the provision of aid, benefits, services, or treatment protected under Title IX. The National Advisory Council on Womens' Educational Programs further defines it according to its place in education as the use of authority to emphasize the sexuality or sexual identity of the student in a manner that prevents or impairs the student' full enjoyment of educational benefits, climate, or opportunities.

Sexual harassment can occur in a variety of forms. Some examples of sexual conduct include: sexual advances; touching of a sexual nature; graffiti of sexual nature; displaying or distributing of sexually explicit drawings, pictures, and written materials; sexual gestures; sexual or dirty jokes; pressure for sexual favors; touching oneself sexually or talking about one's sexual activity in front of others; and spreading rumors about or rating other students as to sexual activity or performance. This conduct must also be unwanted. The victim must be able to show that the conduct is interfering with the victim's receipt of their public education. Prior to the 1970s, sexual harassment was not clearly defined by our legal system; however, in light of Title IX, courts have been forced to clearly define harassment and also establish the precedents for the prevention of future occurrences. *Cannon v. University of Chicago* was the first Supreme Court case to evaluate sexual harassment as sexual discrimination under Title IX. This was the beginning of the courts' evolution in defining and prosecuting sexual harassment cases. In this case, a female student who was denied admission to a medical school sued for sexual discrimination under Title IX. This began the landslide of litigation in this area.

The courts have separated sexual harassment into two categories: quid pro quo and sexually hostile environment. Any form of quid pro quo sexual harassment is illegal under Title IX. This harassment involves an exchange or intent to exchange something for sexual behavior. This would include any use of intimidation or persuasion to instigate sexual conduct in exchange for employment opportunities or academic incentives. Quid pro quo sexual harassment in the educational realm would include sexual favors or sexual relationships in order to acquire better grades or admission to a specific program. Generally, quid pro quo sexual harassment will involve student–teacher, student–administrator contact.

The law further defines sexual harassment in terms of a hostile environment. This type of sexual harassment would include any sexual conduct that is unwarranted on an individual in a severe, persistent, and pervasive manner. According to Title VII of the Civil Rights Act, plaintiffs must be able to prove they were victims of a hostile environment, which is defined as: 1) the plaintiff belongs to a protected group; 2) the plaintiff was subjected to unwelcome sexual harassment; 3) the harassment was based on sex; 4) the harassment affected a term, condition, or privilege of employment; and, 5) the defendant knew or should have known of the harassment and failed to take proper remedial action. Therefore, the employer cannot knowingly allow a hostile environment to endure without taking some type of remedial action. This applies to schools where the hostile environment existed either with teacher–student harassment or student–student harassment and the district knowingly took no action to stop it. In this case, the school district could be held financially liable for damages. As we have already seen, *Franklin v. Gwinnett City Public Schools* was the Supreme Court case that held a school district liable to pay monetary damages when the hostile environment existed and school officials did not take remedial action. This case opened the door for similar cases to seek monetary damages, including *Vance v. Spencer County Public School District and Spencer Board of Education*, where the plaintiff was awarded $220,000 in damages because of prolonged sexual harassment through her high school years.

In the instance of student–teacher sexual harassment cases, there are several factors that need to be considered. First, there needs to be a review of the age of the parties, the relationship inside the school, the number of incidents, the impact on the student, and any signs that the behavior was unwelcome. In addition, after proving that the sexual harassment did indeed occur, the plaintiff must also prove that the school district officials acted with deliberate indifference or did not provide appropriate or adequate action in order to stop the behavior. An example of this type of sexual harassment litigation is *Canty v. Old Rochester Regional School District*. In this case, a coach was accused of raping a student on school premises. Once school officials were notified, they completed a written reprimand. However, he continued to harass the student verbally, which resulted in more written reprimands. Although the courts held that the written reprimands were timely and reasonable measures, they were inadequate as the behavior continued. They further clarified that it is the role of the school officials to take further steps to avoid new liability.

Another example of teacher–student sexual harassment is in *Kinman v. Omaha*. Here, a female teacher began a sexual relationship with a female student who she was insisting was gay. The relationship began when the student was in 10th grade and continued even after the student had graduated. The student became very depressed and attempted to commit suicide. The parents and the student later filed charges against the teacher and the school district seeking monetary damages because they were able to prove there was physical stress experienced by the student as a result of her relationship. Monetary damages were not awarded in this case because the school district was able to demonstrate that it had no knowledge of the relationship and therefore could take no action to stop it.

Student–student sexual harassment is becoming more common. In 1999, a landmark case, *Davis v. Monroe County Board of Education* was heard by the Supreme Court and gave some direction for future cases of this nature.

Davis v. Monroe County Board of Education
526 U.S. 629 (1999)

Topic: Student–Student Sexual Harassment

Facts: The petitioners allege that their fifth-grade daughter, LaShonda, is a victim of sexual harassment by another student in her class. Her classmate attempted to touch LaShonda's breast and genital area and made vulgar statements. Similar conduct occurred in at least three other occasions. These instances were brought to the principal's attention and no disciplinary action was taken.

Issue: Whether the school district is liable under Title VII and Title IX if they were deliberately indifferent to acts of student–student sexual harassment.

Holding: Yes, the school district is liable when they know or should have known of the sexually hostile environment and were deliberately indifferent or did not take appropriate action to address it.

Reasoning:

Major Premise: Schools are responsible for enforcing a policy and providing a safe place that protects students from sexual harassment.

Minor Premise: The school district did not take appropriate action when faced with the presence of a hostile environment.

Conclusion: The school district is guilty of allowing a hostile environment to exist, thus enabling sexual harassment take place and continue.

Notes:

The decision in **Davis** identified a school district's responsibility to prevent a sexually hostile environment from developing. However, the Supreme Court was quick to clarify that any day-to-day childish behavior, such as teasing, shoving, insulting, and others do not qualify as sexual harassment even if it is gender based. They state that the behavior must be "so severe, pervasive, and objectively offensive that it denies its victims the equal access to education that Title IX is designed to protect."

VIII. PRIVACY AND STUDENT RECORDS

The primary purpose of maintaining educational records should be to aid school personnel in maximizing the effectiveness of the educational program for each individual student. A typical student file contains information used for counseling, program development, individualized instruction, grade placement, college admissions, and a variety of other purposes. In addition to certain types of demographic information, student files typically include family background information, health records, progress reports, achievement test results, psychological data, disciplinary records, and other confidential material.

Public Law 93-380, the Family Educational Rights and Privacy Act (FERPA), protects confidentiality of student records. This act, commonly referred to as the Buckley Amendment, was enacted by the Congress in 1974 to guarantee parents and students a certain degree of confidentiality with respect to the maintenance and use of student records. The law is designed to ensure that certain types of personally identifiable information regarding students will not be released without parental consent. If a student is 18 years of age or attends a postsecondary institution, parental consent is not required. In that event, the student has the authority to provide consent. If the student is a dependent, for tax purposes, parents retain a coextensive access right with students over 18 years old. Since P.L. 93-380 is a federal statute, it applies to school districts and schools that receive federal funds. Schools should develop policies and procedures, including a listing of the types and locations of educational records and persons who are responsible for maintaining these records. Copies of these policies and procedures should be made available to parents or students upon request.

Rights of Parents

Parents or legal guardians have the right to inspect their child's record. A school official should be present to assist a parent or guardian in interpreting information contained in the files and to respond to questions that may be raised during the examination process. If the parent challenges the accuracy of any information found in the files, the school must schedule a conference within a reasonable period of time. If the conference does not result in changes to the satisfaction of parents, they may request a hearing with the pupil personnel official to appeal the decision. The parent may also seek relief in civil court. If the student records are subpoenaed by the courts, the parent or eligible student should be contacted prior to the release of records. School officials in another school district in which a student plans to enroll may access that student's records, provided parents or guardians are notified in advance that the records are being transferred to the new district. Students who are 18 years of age have the same rights as their parents regarding the inspection and access to their records.

Rights of School Personnel

Teachers, counselors, and administrators who have a legitimate "right to know" may view student records. A written form, which must be maintained permanently with the file, should indicate specifically what files were reviewed by school personnel and the date in which files were reviewed. Each person desiring access to the file is required to sign this written form. These forms should be available for parents, guardians, or eligible students, since they remain permanently with the file. If challenged, school personnel must demonstrate a legitimate interest in having reviewed the student's file.

In 1994, FERPA was amended to emphasize that institutions are not prevented from maintaining records related to a disciplinary action taken against a student for behavior that posed a significant risk to the student or others. Likewise, institutions are not prevented from disclosing such information to school officials who have been determined to have a legitimate educational interest in the behavior of the student. School districts also are permitted to disclose information regarding disciplinary action to school officials in other schools that have a legitimate educational interest in the behavior of students. The records of minor disciplinary infractions should be destroyed once the student graduates.

Confidentiality and Student Suicide

Closely related to the Buckley Amendment, which provides for confidentiality and privacy regarding student's records, is the right of privacy that is guaranteed by the Fourth Amendment. The relationship between school guidance counselors and the students with whom they interact is determined by these provisions. In protecting the student's privacy, however, many guidance counselors find themselves in a dilemma when the student's behavior may be harmful to either the student or the student's peers. Such a dilemma oftentimes occurs in the instance of students attempting suicide.

It has been contended that school guidance counselors who possess appropriate skills and act in an ethical manner should not be overly concerned about the possibility of lawsuits related to suicide and breaches of privacy. This is in part due to the very real problem of predicting suicidal behavior. However, this attempt at relieving the anxieties of counselors does not confront two important issues: the ethical dilemma of maintaining confidentiality versus the duty to warn, and the potential lack of appropriate training for school counselors in the areas of suicide prevention and intervention. The ethical responsibility of a school counselor or school psychologist to intervene when a student is in danger of hurting himself can be ascertained by examining several legal cases.

Although this case involved a wrongful death action against a psychotherapist who had failed to inform the intended victim of his patient's intent to kill her, *Tarasoff v. The Regents of the University of California* is considered a landmark case that has established that mental health professionals have a legal duty to warn intended victims directly when patients/clients inform the professional of potential harm. In this case, the psychotherapist, a psychologist employed by the University of California at Berkeley, had notified campus police that his patient Prosenjit Poddar had expressed his intention to kill Tatiana Tarasoff. Although the police briefly detained Poddar, he was released and killed Tarasoff approximately two months later. The courts determined that merely informing the police was inadequate. The court ruled that when balancing the potential harms of the violation of the confidentiality of the patient with the potential physical harm to members of society, the therapist must act in a manner to ensure the physical safety of members of society. The Tarasoff decision has been used as a legal and ethical precedent for establishing the psychologist's duty to warn. Although the Tarasoff case does not specifically address a school counselor's duty to warn a parent of their child's suicidal intent, it does provide a framework for understanding how the courts may view the legal liability of mental health professionals when they fail to act to avoid potential harm.

Nicole Eisel was a thirteen-year-old student at Sligo Middle School in Montgomery County, Maryland. Nicole and a friend made a suicide pact. In the week preceding their deaths, Nicole made statements to her friends that she intended to kill herself. The friends reported this to a guidance counselor, who, in turn, told Nicole's guidance counselor. When the two counselors questioned Nicole, she denied any suicide intent. The counselors did not notify the parents or the school administration. Nicole and her friend shot themselves that week with Nicole's father's handgun. Nicole's parents sued the school district, arguing that the counselors and the school were liable for the wrongful death of their daughter because they had not informed the parents of Nicole's intent to commit suicide. The courts found that Nicole's suicide was foreseeable because the counselor had knowledge of her intent to commit suicide from her friends, even though she herself denied it. The courts contended that the counselors had the duty to at least inform the parents by telephone of the possible intent of Nicole to commit suicide (see *Eisel v. Board of Education of Montgomery County* 324 Md. 376: 597 A.2d 447:1991).

In *Wyke v. Polk County School Board* (129 F.3d 560: 1997 U.S. App.; Fla. L. Weekly Fed. C790), Carol Wyke's thirteen-year-old son, Shawn, committed suicide at his home. Shawn twice attempted suicide at school, during school hours. A student told the assistant principal that he had seen Shawn trying to hang himself in a school bathroom. The assistant principal did not tell Shawn's mother about the incident. The next day, Shawn hanged himself at home. It was determined by the court that the "school had negligently failed to supervise Shawn Wyke," and "that the failure was a proximate cause of death." This case once again showed that schools have an obligation to protect their students from harm when it is reasonable to assume that harm is imminent.

However, in questions regarding privacy issues with guidance counselors that involve issues that are not as extreme as a loss of life, the courts have supported the professional judgment of these counselors. In *Roman v. Downingtown School District*, Marjorie Appleby, a school counselor, was charged with invasion of privacy for not properly informing a counselee's parents of the substance of their counseling sessions and for asking improper questions and making inappropriate judgments. Marjorie Appleby conducted a series of approximately eight interviews with Alexander Roman, a tenth-grade student. It was her opinion that he exhibited certain conduct consistent with an "inability to function in reality," a psychosis. The parents were informed that these counseling sessions were being held, but the parents never authorized Appleby during these sessions to question their son and induce responses with respect to his feelings about: his immediate family, including his affection or non-affection or intimate relations for its members; the manner in which his parents had raised him; sex, masturbation, homosexuality, and the "Oedipus complex"; or God, religion, heaven, hell, and sin. During the counseling session, Appleby told Alexander that: his parents were too strict; their religious views were too rigid and conservative; he could not function in reality; he was possibly psychotic; his fears of being a homosexual were normal for his age; and everyone experiences feelings of homosexuality. She ultimately referred him to a school-district psychiatrist for evaluation. When Appleby referred Roman to the psychiatrist, the parents sued for invasion of privacy and violation of the First Amendment Establishment Clause. The courts held that although all of Appleby's behavior may not have been prudent, she was a trained professional with a State certificate to be a guidance counselor, and that she acted within the scope of her duties in making the observations and referrals that she made.

IX. MALPRACTICE

Suits alleging "educational malpractice" have been brought in several states when parents believe that their children have not been provided the level of education ordinarily expected of the grade in which their child was enrolled. But a California court, for example, contended that failure of educational achievement is not an injury within the meaning of tort law. In another decision, *Donohue v. Copiague Union Free School District,* 391 N.E.2d 1352 (N.Y. 1979), New York Court of Appeals also disallowed a cause of action that sought monetary damages for educational malpractice against a school district. The plaintiff alleged that, notwithstanding his receipt of a certificate of graduation, he lacked "the rudimentary ability to comprehend written English on a level sufficient to enable him to complete applications for employment." In its decision the court held that:

> . . . the Constitution places the obligation of maintaining and supporting a system of public schools upon the Legislature. To be sure, this general directive was never intended to impose a duty flowing directly from a local school district to individual pupils to ensure that each pupil receives a minimum level of education, the breach of which duty would entitle a pupil to compensatory damages . . . *Donahue,* 391 N.E.2d at 1443.

X. INSURANCE

In order to reduce the chances of educators being liable for failure to provide reasonable supervision and a safe place for their students, it is important that they be aware of the courts' expectations in this regard. However, to prevent the danger of significant monetary loss due to being found liable for negligence, liability insurance should be obtained. Many educators have such coverage as part of their membership in a professional organization. Individual liability insurance policies are also available for teachers who desire an added degree of security. However, it should be noted that, although professional liability policies cover negligent acts, they rarely cover intentional or criminal acts.

Chapter Three

Schools and the State

This chapter's purpose is to examine the extent of state and local authority when individuals disagree with educational policy involving such issues as compulsory attendance, religion in the schools, use of facilities, aid to non-public schools, school fees, and health services. In these issues the courts attempt to establish a balance between the legitimate demands or objections of individuals toward educational policy and school authorities' perception of their responsibility to the greater population.

I. COMPULSORY ATTENDANCE

A. Satisfied by Parochial, Private, or Home School Attendance

Every state has some form of compulsory education law. These laws usually mandate that children between certain ages must attend some kind of schooling, or they will be found in violation of the law. Central to the legal disputes pertaining to compulsory attendance laws is the balancing of the state's interest in providing students with an appropriate education and the rights of parents to decide when and where their child attends school.

The landmark case on this issue is **Pierce v. Society of Sisters**. In this case, the Supreme Court affirmed the doctrine of compulsory school attendance, but also established the role of parochial and private schools in satisfying the state mandate that children receive schooling.

Pierce v. Soc'y of Sisters of Holy Names
268 U.S. 510, 45 S. Ct. 571, 69 L. Ed. 1070 (1925)

Topic: Compulsory Education

Facts: An Oregon Compulsory Education Act of 1922 ("School Law") requires every child between eight and sixteen years to attend a public school, and failure to do so is declared a misdemeanor. The Society of Sisters ran a private school where children ages between eight and sixteen are taught the subjects usually pursued in Oregon public schools, but with the addition of religious instructions. The School Law caused the withdrawal of children from the private school. The plaintiff sued to prevent enforcement of the School Law.

Issue: Whether the state can order compulsory public school education when an equally adequate, but alternative, form of education exists.

Holding: No, the fundamental theory of liberty embodied in the Fourteenth Amendment excludes any general power of the state to standardize its children by forcing them to accept instruction from public school teachers only. *See Pierce*, 268 U.S. at 535.

Reasoning:

Major Premise: States cannot deprive any person of life, liberty, or property, without due process of law. *See U.S. Const.* amend. XIV, § 1.

Minor Premise: States may have the power to "reasonably . . . regulate all schools, to inspect, supervise and examine them, their teachers and pupils; to require that all children of proper age attend some school . . ." *Pierce*, 268 U.S. at 534 (dictum).

Conclusion: The Oregon Compulsory Education Act of 1922 deprived private schools of their property interest (by denying the right of schools and teachers to engage in a useful business or profession). *See Pierce*, 268 U.S. at 532, 534. The Act also deprived parents their liberty interest (the right of parents to choose schools where their children will receive appropriate mental and religious training). *See Id.* at 532, 534–35.

Notes and Questions

The challenged Oregon law in *Pierce* had been promoted primarily by members of the Ku Klux Klan and Oregon's Scottish Rite Masons. Their actions were evidence of xenophobic response on the part of some Americans after World War I to ensure that children would be properly socialized in the tenets of Americanism.

An Amish group contested Wisconsin's compulsory attendance law that required attendance at a public or private school until age sixteen. The Amish did not want their children to attend either a public or private high school after the eighth grade because they considered such schools to be "worldly." A Supreme Court decision upheld the Amish position on several grounds. The Court contended that enforcing the state law would gravely endanger, if not destroy, the free exercise of Amish religious beliefs. Additionally, the Court's decision was influenced not only by the group's nearly three hundred years of existence but also by the perception that, although perhaps unconventional, the Amish had evidenced a highly successful social unit characterized by members who were model citizens. See *Wisconsin v. Yoder*, 406 U.S. 205 (1972).

A Pentecostal parent who objected to sending his children to public schools was not upheld. The court ruled that the state's interest in compulsory attendance overrides the parent's interest in avoiding exposure to the unisex movement, secular humanism, and medical care. See *Duro v. District Attorney, Second Judicial District of North Carolina*, 712 F.2d 96 (4th Cir. 1983, *cert. Denied*, 465 U.S. 1006 [1984]).

B. Regulation of Nonpublic Schools

After the **Pierce** decision established the fact that private school attendance could satisfy a state's compulsory attendance laws, the question then arose as to the extent that the state could regulate nonpublic schools. The Supreme Court addressed this issue in *Farrington v. Tokushige*, 273 U.S. 284 (1926).

Farrington resulted from a state attempt to Americanize students in Hawaii in the Japanese foreign-language schools on the islands. The contested regulations required teachers in these schools to possess "ideals of democracy," knowledge of American history, and fluency in English. Additionally, they restricted hours of operation, established entrance requirements, and prescribed textbooks. These regulations, the Court held, served no demonstrable public interest, but instead amounted to a deliberate plan of strict governmental control, infringing on the rights of both parents and school owners.

Both **Pierce** and *Farrington,* therefore, reflect a philosophy that parents should have freedom of choice in the education of their children. Moreover, in sanctioning what many people feared was subversive, these decisions affirm a faith in the sustaining power of American tolerance.

Regulation of private schools varies among the states. Some states require that the quality of education provided by the private school be essentially equivalent to that provided in the public schools. This may include a requirement for certified teachers and certain course offerings. Other states merely have regulations dealing primarily with health, safety, and sanitation.

In recent years, state regulation of religious private schools has received court attention. These schools frequently allege that their First Amendment religious freedom is being restricted. Courts have tended to reject these challenges to minimal instructional programs and requirements that teachers have baccalaureate degrees. See *Nebraska v. Faith Baptist Church,* 301 N.W.2d 571 (1981), *Bangor Baptist Church v. Maine,* 549 F.Supp. 1208 (Me.1982), *North Dakota v. Shaver,* 294 N.W.2d 883 (N.D. 1981), and *North Dakota v. Rivinius,* 328 N.W.2d 220 (N.D. 1982).

A. Home Instruction

Parents frequently decide to instruct their children at home because of dissatisfaction with both public and non-public schools. This type of instruction is generally allowed, but some states require the home program to be essentially equivalent to that offered in the public schools, while others require a qualified teacher to give the instruction. In most states, the burden of demonstrating that the same instruction is substantially equivalent to that offered in the public schools is on the parents. See *New Jersey v. Massa*, 231 A.2d 252 (N.J. Sup. Ct. 1967), in which the court held that equivalent education other than in a public school requires only a showing of academic equivalence.

II. RELIGION IN THE SCHOOLS

The Supreme Court and lower federal courts have consistently declared that Bible reading, prayer, and other forms of religious activities in public schools during normal operating hours is unconstitutional. However, these decisions do not preclude this issue from remaining highly controversial and emotional. Consequently, there has been a persistent stream of litigation focusing on church–state relations.

In an effort to ensure a separation of church and state, the framers of the Constitution included the following language in the First Amendment: "Congress shall make no law respecting an establishment of religion, or prohibiting the free exercise thereof." On the basis of these words, the courts must determine the constitutionality of such questions as allowing prayer and Bible reading in the public schools during normal school hours or at graduation exercises, conducting baccalaureate services, permitting Bible study or other religious clubs, disseminating Bibles or other religious writings, or observing religious holidays.

A. School-Sponsored Prayer and Bible Reading

In the early 1960s, two Supreme Court decisions established the precedent pertaining to prayer in public schools. In **Engel v. Vitale**, the Court held that recitation of a prayer composed by the New York State Board of Regents, which was to be said in the presence of a teacher at the beginning of the school day, was unconstitutional and in violation of the establishment clause of the First Amendment.

In **School District of Abington Township v. Schempp**, the Court held that reading the Bible for sectarian purposed and reciting the Lord's Prayer in public schools during normal school hours were unconstitutional. However, the Court said that the Bible could be read as literature in an appropriate class, such as a comparative religion class. Despite these decisions, prayer in some public schools did not stop. The issue has remained highly charged and continues to be one of national political debate.

After **Schempp**, the Supreme Court did not directly address the issue again until *Wallace v. Jaffree*, 472 U.S. 38 (1985). This six-to-three decision held that the setting aside of classroom time for school-sponsored silent prayer, which was authorized in sixteen states at the time of the decision, was unconstitutional. A careful reading of the decision suggests that allowing for a moment of silence, which was authorized in nine states, may be constitutional. According to Justice O'Connor, who wrote a concurring opinion, the crucial question regarding a moment of silence is "whether the state has conveyed or attempted to convey the message that children should use the moment of silence for prayer."

The United States Supreme Court again addressed a school prayer issue in *Lee v. Weisman* in 1992. In this case, the court held that prayers at graduation exercises were unconstitutional.

1. Recitation of a State Prayer

Engel v. Vitale
370 U.S. 421, 82 S. Ct. 1261, 8 L. Ed. 2d 601

Topic: Recitation of a State Prayer

Facts: The State of New York adopted a program of daily recitation of prayers in public schools. Although the prayers were denominationally neutral, and student participation is voluntary, parents of ten pupils brought an action to challenge the constitutionality of the program as violative of the First Amendment. That provision of the First Amendment commands that Congress shall make no law respecting an establishment of religion, and this provision is applicable to the states through the Fourteenth Amendment.

Issue: Whether, by using its public school system to encourage recitation of the prayers, the State of New York has adopted a practice wholly inconsistent with the Establishment Clause.

Holding: Yes, the Establishment Clause does not require any showing of governmental compulsion and is violated by the adoption of laws that establish an official religion, whether or not those laws operate directly to coerce non-observing individuals. *See Engel*, 370 U.S. at 430. Therefore, the State's school prayer program is prohibited by the Establishment Clause.

Reasoning:

Major Premise: The Establishment Clause of the First Amendment bars government from controlling or supporting religion and religious activity.

Minor Premise: The recitation of an official school prayer advances religion, and channels religious activity by requiring and promoting religious expression.

Conclusion: The Establishment Clause bars the practice of reciting an official, state-sanctioned school prayer.

2. Prayer and Bible Reading

School Dist. of Abington Township v. Schempp
Murray v. Curlett
374 U.S. 203, 83 S. Ct. 1560, 10 L. Ed. 2d 844 (1963)

Topic: Prayer and Bible Reading in Public Schools

Facts: A Pennsylvania statute required the reading, at the opening of each school day, of verses from the Bible and the recitation of the Lord's Prayer by the students in unison. Maryland adopted a similar statute in 1905. The students and their parents were advised that the students may absent himself or herself from the classroom. Plaintiffs in both cases seek to prevent the enforcement of the statutes.

Issue: Whether the Establishment Clause of the First Amendment, protecting freedom of religion, was violated by the Pennsylvania and Maryland statutes requiring prayer and Bible readings in state public schools.

Holding: Yes, the purpose and primary effect of a state statute must neither advance nor inhibit religion. *See Schempp*, 374 U.S. at 222. The statutes in this case violated the Establishment Clause of the First Amendment.

Reasoning:

Major Premise: States cannot make any laws respecting an establishment of religion. See *Schempp*, 374 U.S. at 215–16.

Minor Premise: By mandating readings from the Bible and recitation of the Lord's Prayer, the state violates the required position of neutrality.

Conclusion: The state, by mandating school prayer and Bible readings, is advancing religion. In light of the Establishment Clause of the First Amendment, as applied to the States by the Fourteenth Amendment, the statutes are unconstitutional.

Notes

The notion of the separation of church and state that we espouse in the United States is not shared in many other countries. Religion is only grudgingly tolerated in communist countries like Cuba. In England, the Church of England and that country's monarch, as its head, is the official religion. Many Latin countries' laws are based on Catholic Church dogma. And teachings from the *Koran* not only underpin governmental policy in Islamic countries, but religious leaders often exert enormous political and societal influence. Germany, for example, has a national church tax of 9% imposed on income derived from wages and salaries. Belgium, like many of these countries, has an extensive aid to nonpublic schools program.

Suppose every child in a public school classroom voted to begin each class with a prayer and Bible reading. Would this lift any constitutional barriers? Is there a difference if a local school board or state statute authorized such practices?

Courts apply what is known as the *Lemon Test* to First Amendment establishment clause cases. This test was first enunciated in *Lemon v. Kurtzman,* 403 U.S. 602 (1971) to assist the courts in determining whether the state had stepped over the "wall of separation" of church and state. Under this test, to satisfy the Establishment Clause, a governmental practice must (1) reflect a clearly secular purpose; (2) have a primary effect that neither advances nor inhibits religion; and (3) avoid excessive entanglement with religion. One can readily see how in the cases regarding prayer in public schools, one or another of the steps in the *Lemon Test* has been violated.

Another nuance of this issue is how the courts look at holiday displays. The Supreme Court ruled in a five-to-four decision that a Christmas nativity scene placed in a county court house violated the Establishment Clause. However, an 18-foot Chanukah menorah, which was placed just outside a city-county building next to the city's 45-foot Christmas tree, and a sign saluting liberty, was declared not to violate the Establishment Clause. The combined display, the Court reasoned, was recognition that both Christmas and Chanukah are part of the same winter-holiday season. See *Allegheny v. American Civil Liberties Union*, 492 U.S. 573 (1989). Five years earlier, in a five-to-four decision, a forty-year practice of having a nativity scene in a park owned by a nonprofit organization had been upheld by the Court. See *Lynch v. Donnelly,* 465 U.S. 668 (1984). These close and seemingly contradictory decisions and the often-acrimonious language in the individual opinions reveal a wide divergence among several of the justices regarding separation of church and state issues.

3. Prayers at Graduation Exercises and other Public School Activities

Since the **Engel** case, many lower courts have been asked to rule on the constitutionality of invocations and benedictions at graduation exercise and prayer at other school-sponsored activities outside the classroom. In a dramatic five-to-four decision, the Court in **Lee v. Weisman** ruled that prayers at graduation exercises were unconstitutional.

Lee v. Weisman
505 U.S. 577, 112 S. Ct. 2649, 120 L. Ed. 2d 467 (1992)

Topic: Prayers at Graduation Exercises

Facts: The Rhode Island school district permitted middle school and high school principals, at their discretion, to invite clergymen to offer invocations and benedictions at graduation ceremonies. A middle school principal invited a rabbi to offer prayers at the graduation ceremonies and advised him that the prayers at the school should be "nonsectarian." The father of a graduating student sued the school district, claiming a violation of the Establishment Clause of the First Amendment.

Issue: Whether including clerical members who offer prayers violates the Religion Clauses of the First Amendment, provisions of the Fourteenth Amendment makes applicable with full force to the states and their school districts.

Holding: Yes, invocations or benedictions led by a clergy at an official public school graduation ceremony violate the Establishment Clause of the First Amendment.

Reasoning:

Major Premise: The Federal Constitution guarantees that government may not coerce anyone to support or participate in religion or religious exercises, or otherwise act in a way which "establishes" a religion. *See Lee*, 505 U.S. at 587.

Minor Premise: Although the school does not require attendance as a condition for receipt of the diploma, a student's participation in graduation ceremonies is, in a fair and real sense, obligatory. *See Lee*, 505 U.S. at 586.

Conclusion: State-sanctioned prayers during graduation ceremonies violate the Establishment Clause of the First Amendment.

Notes and Questions

Since the Supreme Court has had a number of "conservative" appointees in recent years, it was believed that this decision would become the precedent for changing the legal rules regarding prayer in public schools. To the contrary, in addition to clearly revealing the basic philosophic differences regarding this issue, the majority, concurring, and dissenting opinions also reveal the high degree of acrimony among the justices on this issue.

B. Equal Access

A number of public schools have Bible or other religious study groups that meet on school grounds outside of the school day. In many instances, they have been recognized as official school organizations and have often advertised their activities on bulletin boards or through the school newspaper.

These meetings have been the subject of much litigation and, in an attempt to address the issue, Congress in 1984 passed the Equal Access Act. Under this act, it is unlawful for a public secondary school that receives federal financial assistance and has created a limited open forum to deny recognition of student-initiated groups on the basis of the religious, political, or philosophical content of the speech at meetings. Although faculty members may be present, they may not participate, and outsiders may not control or regularly attend group meetings. The law declares that a limited open forum has been created when one or more non-curricular student groups are allowed to meet on school premises during non-instructional time. A limited open forum is not created when the clubs are curriculum oriented.

C. The Teaching of Evolution

The "Scopes monkey trial" in 1925 focused the nation's attention on the topic of teaching evolution in the nation's schools. Although John Scopes was found guilty of teaching evolution, and his conviction was overturned on a technicality, the issue remained dormant until the 1970s. By then, Darwin's theory of evolution was routinely taught in most public schools as the "origin of the species." At that time, however, "fundamentalist" groups opposed to the teaching of evolution developed a new strategy, which sought to establish that the Biblical account of creation is a respectable scientific theory and deserves public classroom time for its teaching. Although debated in several legislatures, creationism, as the theory became known, was enacted into law in Arkansas and Louisiana. These statutes were quickly challenged on the basis of their constitutionality. In **Edwards v. Aguillard,** the United States Supreme Court declared the practice as violative of the First Amendment's prohibition against establishment of religion.

Edwards v. Aguillard
482 U.S. 578, 107 S. Ct. 2573, 96 L. Ed. 2d 510 (1987)

Topic: Teaching of Evolution in Public Schools

Facts: A Louisiana statute (Creationism Act) required the state public school to give a "balanced treatment" of "creation science" and "evolution science." The statute forbids the teaching of the theory of evolution in public schools unless accompanied by instruction in "creation science."

Issue: Whether the Creationism Act violates the Establishment Clause of the First Amendment.

Holding: Yes, the Act violates the Establishment Clause of the First Amendment because it is designed to either promote the theory of "creation science" that embodies a particular religious tenet or to prohibit the teaching of a scientific theory opposed by certain religious sects. *See Edwards*, 482 U.S. at 593.

Reasoning:

Major Premise: The teaching of religion violates the Establishment Clause of the First Amendment.

Minor Premise: The Creationism Act either prohibits the teaching of the "evolution theory" or it requires the teaching of "creation science" with the purpose of advancing a particular religious doctrine.

Conclusion: The Creationism Act is unconstitutional because it advances a religious doctrine in violation of the Establishment Clause of the First Amendment.

B. Textbooks

Textbooks can be the subject of court cases on the grounds that certain books promote secular humanism and inhibit theistic religion. In one instance, parents charged that history, social studies, and home economics books promoted secular humanism by excluding facts about religion and by failing to present a Biblically based or divine framework for decision making. The Eleventh United States Circuit Court of Appeals did not uphold the parents' contentions. See *Smith v. Board of School Commissioners of Mobile County,* 827 F.2d 684 (11th Cir. 1987).

Secular humanism is a belief that one should act with civility toward another simply because both parties are human beings. In other words, the basic for morality is our basic humanity. This is contrasted with the theistic view that a Supreme Being is the reason for and the source of the moral code. In *Smith*, the court held that the textbooks were neutral toward religion and did not espouse secular humanism, or any other religion. The plaintiffs argued that by not mentioning a Supreme Being somewhere in the text, the authors were espousing secular humanism by default.

C. Distribution of Religious Literature

One of the earliest decisions regarding the distribution of Bibles and other religious literature in public school is *Tudor v. Board of Education of Borough of Rutherford,* 100 A.2d 857 (N.J.1953). In this court case, the distribution of Gideon Bibles was prohibited. In an earlier decision, a policy that allowed all religions to distribute their literature was upheld. In this instance, although literature could not be distributed by going from classroom to classroom or by walking up and down aisles, it could be distributed at a designated place. See *Meltzer v. Board of Public Instruction of Orange County,* 577 F.2d 311 (5th Cir. 1978). Another court did not uphold the distribution of sectarian literature such as leaflets advertising religious activities. See *Hernandez v. Hanson,* 430 F.Supp. 1154 (Neb. 1977). It should be noted that allowing one religious group to distribute its literature opens a forum for such distribution that cannot be closed to groups that are often objects of community disdain, such as Satanists.

D. Shared Time and Religious Instruction

In *McCollum v. Board of Education of School District No. 71,*333 U. S. 203 (1948), the Supreme Court invalidated a plan under which separate Protestant, Catholic, and Jewish religious classes were taught in the public school buildings. The court contended that the use of tax-supported property for religious instruction, the close cooperation between school authorities and religious officials, and the use of the state's compulsory education system all tended to promote religious education, and, therefore, violated the First Amendment. In another decision, *Zorach v. Clauson,* 343 U.S. 306 (1952), the Court upheld a plan whereby students were released during public school hours to attend religious instruction classes on the school premises.

Several cases have addressed the issue of shared time. In one case, a public school would not enroll a parochial school student in a band course at the public school. The public school had a policy of allowing attendance in its schools only by full-time students. See *Snyder v. Charlotte Public School District,* 365 N.W.2d 151 (Mich. 1984), in which the Michigan Supreme Court ruled that public schools must open "nonessential elective courses" such as band, art, driver's education, and advanced mathematics to private-school students.

In *Pulido v. Cavazos,* 934 F.2d 912 (8th Cir. 1991), Chapter 1 remedial educational services to low-income parochial school students may be provided at on-site locations if they are conducted in religiously neutral settings. Heretofore, such services could only be provided off-premise.

G. Religious Holidays

Since the courts have consistently cautioned school systems from favoring one religion over another, closing schools on Christian holidays such as Christmas, Easter, and Good Friday has received much attention. Christmas has generally been acknowledged to have sufficient secular connotations to warrant closing the schools during that holiday, but Easter and Good Friday have not been similarly viewed. Consequently, many school systems wishing to continue having a break in the spring have renamed their Easter break as spring break. See *Metzl v. Leininger,* 850 F. Supp. 740 (Ill. 1994). In this case, the court held that holding no classes on Good Friday was a violation of the First Amendment.

E. Accommodation of Religion

Because our nation was founded by the Pilgrims and Puritans who were settling here in pursuit of religious freedom, our culture is steeped in religious traditions and customs. This historical context has been acknowledged and recognized by the courts in its decisions regarding religious practices in our society. Hence, there are times that the courts made decisions that on the surface seem inconsistent, but are, in effect, accommodations to religion and its historical and cultural importance in our society. For example, the courts have allowed a prayer offered by alternating clergymen and women to begin each Congressional session. On the surface, this would seem inconsistent with the prayer in public school rulings that we have just reviewed. However, in light of the fact that we are dealing with adults in Congress and because of the importance of religion in our culture, the courts have allowed this practice to continue.

Another more topical instance of an accommodation of religion by the courts is the inclusion of the word "God" in the pledge of allegiance. The use of this word in the pledge was challenged by Dr. Michael Newdow, an avowed atheist, as a violation of the Establishment Clause of the First Amendment. Dr. Newdow is an emergency-room physician with a law degree who argued that the school district was unconstitutionally exposing his 10-year-old daughter to religious dogma during the daily classroom ritual of pledging allegiance to the American flag.

In *Elk Grove Unified School District v. Newdow*, Chief Justice Rehnquist and the Supreme Court ruled that "... Reciting the pledge, or listening to others recite it, is a patriotic exercise, not a religious one; participants promise fidelity to our flag and our nation, not to any particular God, faith, or church." Justice O'Connor commented that "... It is unsurprising that a nation founded by religious refugees and dedicated to religious freedom should find references to divinity in its symbols, songs, mottoes, and oaths ..." Thus, this is a typical instance of the courts "accommodating" religion.

III. USE OF FACILITIES

The procedure that has evolved from case law concerning the use of school facilities suggests that if facilities are to be leased to one type of group, they must be available to all within the group. However, such use may be denied if (1) the user fails or refuses to abide by reasonable rules and regulations pertaining to the use, (2) there is a demonstrated danger of violence or disruption associated with meetings of this particular group, or (3) the meeting violates a local ordinance, or either state or federal constitutional provisions of law. It should be noted that in the absence of a state statute mandating their use, local systems are not obligated to make school buildings available for public activities.

Although allowing buildings to be used for social, civic, and recreational meetings outside of school hours, many school systems, fearing lawsuits, have not allowed their buildings to be used for religious purposes. Such restrictions resulted in many lawsuits brought by churches and religious organizations, over the years, claiming unfair treatment. Although not specifically addressing the issue of after-hours church use, a unanimous Supreme Court decision in **Lamb's Chapel v. Center Moriches Union Free School District** ruled that a church should be allowed to show, after normal school hours on school premises, a family-oriented movie that presented views about family issues and child rearing from a Christian perspective.

Lamb's Chapel v. Ctr. Moriches Union Free Sch. Dist.
508 U.S. 384, 113 S. Ct. 2141, 124 L. Ed. 2d 352 (1993)

Topic: Use of Public School Facilities

Facts: A New York State law authorizes local school boards to adopt reasonable regulations for the use of school property for 10 specified purposes when the property is not in use for school purposes. Among the permitted uses is the holding of "social, civic, and recreational meetings and entertainments," but the list of permitted uses does not include meetings for religious purposes. Lamb's Chapel wanted to use the school facilities, after school hours, to show family-oriented movies that presented views about family issues and child-rearing from a religious standpoint. This meeting is open to the public. The school district twice denied Lamb's Chapel's application on the ground that the film series appeared to be church related.

Issue: Whether the school board violated the Free Speech Clause of the First Amendment by denying a church access to school premises to exhibit for public viewing and for religious purposes a film series dealing with family and child-rearing issues.

Holding: Yes, since the film series would not have been shown during school hours, would not have been sponsored by the school, and would have been open to the public, "there would have been no realistic danger that the community would think that the [school] District was endorsing religion or any particular creed, and any benefit to the Church would have been no more than incidental." *Lamb's Chapel*, 508 U.S. at 395.

Reasoning:

Major Premise: The First Amendment forbids the government from regulating speech in ways that favor some viewpoints at the expense of others. *See Lamb's Chapel*, 508 U.S. at 394.

Minor Premise: Permitting the school property to be used to exhibit the film series would not be an establishment of religion because the use of the facility has a secular purpose, does not have the effect of advancing or inhibiting religion, and it does not foster an "excessive entanglement" with religion. *See Lamb's Chapel*, 508 U.S. at 395. The film series was denied solely because the film dealt with the subject from a religious standpoint. *Id*. at 394.

Conclusion: Lamb Chapel's First Amendment rights under the Free Speech Clause were violated because it has the right to present a point of view on the subject, in a public forum, from a religious standpoint.

IV. AID TO NONPUBLIC SCHOOLS

Nationally, approximately 12% of American students attend nonpublic schools. In some states, that figure approaches the 50% mark. About 70% of the nonpublic schools are Catholic schools, and about 15% of nonpublic school students attend non-church related schools. Legislatures in several states having large numbers of nonpublic school students have passed measures that have attempted to financially assist the nonpublic school sector. Because these measures have raised serious questions pertaining to the proper separation of church and state under the First Amendment, their constitutionality has been examined by the Supreme Court.

In *Lemon v. Kurtzman*, 403 U.S. 602 (1971) the Court struck down both an attempt by the Rhode Island legislature to provide a 15% salary supplement to be paid to those teachers dealing with secular subjects in nonpublic schools and a Pennsylvania statute that provided financial support to nonpublic elementary and secondary schools by way of reimbursement for the cost of teachers' salaries, textbooks, and instructional materials in specified secular subjects. The Court held that the "cumulative impact of the entire relationship arising under the statutes in each state involves excessive entanglement between government and religion." Furthermore, the Court reasoned that these state programs had divisive political potential that would be a threat to the normal political process. Because candidates would be forced to declare their position on amounts of money to be expended in such programs, political division along religious lines would develop. The Court contended that this was a principal evil that the First Amendment was intended to protect against. This case provided the courts with the Lemon Test (page 32).

Levitt v. Committee for Public Education and Religious Liberty, 413 U.S. 472 (1973) was a case where a New York statute was struck down by the Supreme Court. Under this statute, nonpublic schools would have been reimbursed for expenses incurred in administering, grading, compiling, and reporting test results: maintaining pupil attendance and health records; recording qualifications and characteristics of personnel; and preparing and submitting various reports to the state. The Court ruled that such aid would have the primary purpose of effect of advancing religion or religious education and that it would lead to excessive entanglement between church and state. Both of these conditions would violate the *Lemon Test.*

However, in *Committee for Public Education and Religious Liberty v. Regan,* 442 U.S. 928 (1980), the Court upheld a revised version of the law that had been declared unconstitutional in *Levitt.* The revised law allowed the state to reimburse private schools, including sectarian schools, for the expenses connected with keeping official attendance and other records, for administering three state tests, and for grading two of the tests.

In *Committee for Public Education and Religious Liberty v. Nyquist,* 413 U.S. 756 (1973), which provided for the maintenance and repair of nonpublic school facilities, tuition reimbursement for parents of nonpublic school students, and tax relief for those not qualifying for tuition reimbursement, another New York law was invalidated by the Court. And a Pennsylvania law providing for parent reimbursement for nonpublic school students was also invalidated in *Sloan v. Lemon,* 413 U.S. 825 (1973). The majority opinion declared that there was no constitutionally significant difference between Pennsylvania's tuition grant system and New York's tuition reimbursement program, which was held in violation of the Establishment Clause in *Nyquist.* You will notice that most of these cases took place in large cities and in states where there was a significant Catholic population and a large number of Catholic schools.

In *Meek v. Pittenger,* 421 U.S. 349 (1975), the Court was asked to rule on a Pennsylvania statute that provided for auxiliary services for exceptional, remedial, or educationally disadvantaged nonpublic school students; for lending instructional materials and equipment to nonpublic schools; and for lending textbooks to nonpublic school students. The Court invalidated all but the textbook loan provision of the Pennsylvania law. It held that the act had the unconstitutional primary effect of advancing religion because of the predominantly religious character of the benefiting schools. Additionally, the Court stated that the act provided excessive opportunities for political fragmentation and division along religious lines.

In another decision, *Wolman v. Walter,* 433 U.S. 229 (1977), the Court addressed the constitutionality of an Ohio statute that had attempted to conform to the *Meek* ruling. The decision, which revealed wide disagreement among the justices, held that the provisions providing nonpublic students with books, standardized testing and scoring, diagnostic services, and therapeutic and remedial services were constitutional. However, provisions relating to instructional materials and equipment and field trip services were held to be unconstitutional. The Court was now more clearly distinguishing between a "child benefit," which was constitutional, and a "school benefit," which was not.

In *Mueller v. Allen,* 463 U.S. 388 (1983), the court upheld a Minnesota law permitting taxpayers to claim a deduction from gross income on their state income tax for expenses incurred for "tuition, textbooks, and transportation" not exceeding $500 for dependents in grades K–6 and $700 for dependents in grades 7–12. A distinction between this decision and Court's 1973 *Nyquist* ruling appears to be that *Nyquist* rejected a tax *credit* for parents whose children attended nonpublic school, while *Mueller* allowed a tax *deduction* for all parents, including those whose children attended public schools. The tax deduction, the majority reasoned, was simply part of the state's tax law permitting deductions for a number of items. The dissenter argued that the difference between a tax credit and a deduction was "a distinction without a difference," and that 90% of private school students were in sectarian schools. The *Mueller* decision gives hope to those who are in favor of using educational vouchers.

The "Child Benefit" theory was first established in 1947, when the Supreme Court upheld the constitutionality of providing transportation to parochial school students in *Everson v. Board of Education of Township of Ewing,* 330 U.S. 1 (1947). More than thirty years later, a Rhode Island statute providing for the busing of students to nonpublic school was held not to violate state or federal constitutional provisions. See *Members of the Jamestown School Committee v. Schmidt,* 405 A.2d 16 (R.I. 1979).

Under the Internal Revenue Code, tax exemptions may be granted to "corporations . . . organized and operated exclusively for religious, charitable . . . or educational purposes." A private religious university was devoted to the teaching and propagation of fundamentalist religious beliefs, which included that God intended segregation of the races and that scripture forbids interracial dating and marriage. Students were expelled if they did not follow these prohibitions. The Internal Revenue Service, upheld by the Supreme Court, withdrew the college's tax exempt status, having determined that the racial policy was not "charitable" as required by the Code. See *Bob Jones University v. United States,* 461 A.2d 16 (R.I. 1979).

The Court struck down the used of federal education funds under Chapter I (formerly Title I of the Elementary and Secondary Education Act) to pay public school teachers who taught in programs aimed at helping low-income, educationally deprived students in parochial schools. See *Aguiler v. Felton,* 473 U.S. 402 (1985). In 1997, however, the Court reversed itself and allowed public school teachers to offer these remedial services on parochial school property and in parochial school classrooms. This reversed the original 1985 ruling that relegated such classes to mobile vans and trailers. See *Agostino v. Felton,* 567 U.S. 560 (1997).

V. SCHOOL FEES

The charging of school fees by public schools for such items as supplies, extracurricular activities, transportation to school, and texts is a controversial issue. The California Supreme Court considered the issue of charging fees for extracurricular activities in **Hartzell v. Connell.**

Hartzell v. Connell
679 P.2d 35 (Cal. 1984)

Topic: School Fees

Facts: A California school district imposed a $25 fee on students for participation in specific extracurricular activities. Participation in a wide variety of other extracurricular activities is available free of charge and open to any student. The District also adopted a fee-waiver policy based on student financial need in an attempt to ensure that the fees imposed would not prevent a student from participating. A taxpayer with two children in public schools and a grouping of community organizations sued the school district, claiming that imposition of the fees violated the free school guarantee of the California Constitution. *See* Cal. CONST. art. 9, § 5.

Issue: Whether extracurricular activities fall within the free education guaranteed by the Constitution; if so, whether the imposition of a fee for participation in extracurricular activities, even with a waiver provision, violates the Constitution.

Holding: All educational activities, curricular or extracurricular, offered to students by the school district fall within the free school guarantee of article IX, section 5 of the Constitution. *See Hartzell* 679 P.2d at 43. The fee-waiver policy, based on financial hardship, is no defense to a violation of the free school guarantee. *Id.* at 44.

Reasoning:

Major Premise: Extracurricular activities constitute an integral component of public education.

Minor Premise: All educational activities, curricular or extracurricular, fall within the free school guarantee of the California Constitution.

Conclusion: Imposition of fees for participation in extracurricular activities violates the free school guarantee of the California Constitution.

Notes and Questions

May a student's transcript be withheld for failure to pay school fees? This is often an issue in nonpublic schools when a student does not pay his or her tuition. See *Paulson v. Minidoka County School District No.331,* 463 P.2d

935 (Idaho 1970), where the court stated that "free common schools" were not being provided when access to official reports of students' records depended upon payment of a $25 unconstitutional school fee. In the case of unpaid tuition in nonpublic schools, the courts have usually dealt with this issue under contract law. If the school has provided the service, but the student has not paid for the service, the student and not the school has breached the conditions of the contract. Thus, withholding transcripts may be appropriate.

VI. HEALTH SERVICES

In recent years, many parents have objected to school systems that have attempted to impose health services on students, especially in the areas of immunization and the distribution of condoms for disease prevention.

A. Immunization

Immunization is ordinarily upheld by the courts, with the exception of such state statutes that contain an exemption for those whose religious beliefs preclude vaccination.

Brown v. Stone
378 So. 2d 218 (Miss. 1979)

Topic: Immunization

Facts: According to a Mississippi law, it shall be unlawful for any child to attend school without being vaccinated against diseases, as specified by the State Health Officer. A certificate of religious exemption from vaccination may be offered on behalf of a child by an officer of a church of a recognized denomination. A father challenged the law on the grounds that it violated the First Amendment of the United States Constitution protecting the free exercise of religion, since it forced him to join a "recognized religious denomination."

Issue: Whether the religious exemption from vaccination violated the Constitution when it allows an exemption on behalf of a child by an officer of a church of a recognized denomination.

Holding: Yes, the religious exemption of the Mississippi statute discriminates against the great majority of children whose parents do not hold such religious convictions. *See Brown*, 378 So. 2d at 223. This results in a violation of the Fourteenth Amendment to the United States Constitution providing for equal protection of the laws, since it would "require the great body of school children to be vaccinated and at the same time expose them to the hazard of associating in school with children exempted under the religious exemption . . ." *Id.*

Reasoning:

Major Premise: The Fourteenth Amendment guarantees equal protection under the law.

Minor Premise: Allowing children to enroll in school without immunization would violate the Fourteenth Amendment rights of those children who were immunized.

Conclusion: To give effect to the religious exemption of the Mississippi statute would require a majority of the children to be vaccinated, yet expose them to the hazard of associating in school with children who are exempted under the religious exemption and who had not been immunized. Therefore, the statute violated the Fourteenth Amendment rights of those children who were immunized.

For a contrary view on this issue, see *Berg v. Glen Cove City School District*, where an exemption was allowed on religious belief grounds.

Berg v. Glen Cove City School District
873 F. Supp. 651 (New York, 1994)

Topic: Immunization

Facts: Kathryn and David Berg sought to enroll their five-year-old twin daughters, Emily and Sasha, in the Glen Cove City School District, and requested exemption from the immunization requirement of New York State. The Bergs claimed such an exemption on religious grounds. They were Jewish but argued that their personal religious beliefs did not permit them to use unnatural substances to thwart diseases.

Issue: Whether the Free Exercise Clause of the First Amendment allows parents not to comply with immunization laws.

Holding: Yes, in many cases the Free Exercise Clause is considered more important than the responsibility of the school district to provide a safe place for its students.

Reasoning:

Major Premise: Schools have the right to impose immunization policies in their efforts to provide a safe place for their students.

Minor Premise: Parents have a right to object to immunization if it violates their religious beliefs.
Conclusion: In this case, the rights of the parents superceded the rights of the school district.

B. Distribution of Condoms

Some urban school systems have attempted to address problems of teenage pregnancy and the AIDS epidemic by making condoms available to students. Condom distribution to high school students upon request was litigated in *Alfonso v. Fernandez*, 606 N.Y.S. 2d 259 (N.Y. App. Div. 1993). In its decision, the court declared that since the program was a "health issue" the school district could not dispense condoms without the prior consent of parents or without an option not to participate. Additionally, the court contended that the plan violated the parents' due process rights under the Fourteenth Amendment to rear their children as they see fit. The program, however, did not violate the parents' or students' free exercise of religion.

Chapter Four

Students and the Law

Prior to the 1970s, the courts usually upheld school authorities even if they demonstrated no more than the *reasonability* of their actions. Public schools were perceived as enjoying parental prerogatives, and it was uncertain whether constitutional rights extended to students. However, in a 1969 landmark decision, the United States Supreme Court declared that students do not "shed their constitutional rights to freedom of speech or expression at the schoolhouse gate." Subsequently, in 1975, the high court held that public school students possess liberty and property interest in their education, and therefore, that constitutional principles of due process apply to school officials' treatment of students. Several important federal statutes also emerged in the early 1970s, further expanding the scope of student rights.

In the mid-1980s, however, the courts shifted their tendency to uphold students rights and began deciding in favor of the school districts. Several Supreme Court decisions since then clearly increased the authority of public school officials regarding student rights. An examination of court decisions in these areas reveals that courts often must balance student's constitutional rights against the duty of public school officials to maintain an appropriate environment for learning and safety.

I. FREEDOM OF EXPRESSION

A. The Tinker Doctrine

Tinker v. Des Moines Independent Community School District changed forever the way the courts viewed student rights, especially freedom of speech and expression. Although the seven-to-two decision did not address the question of "pure speech" (the issue before the Court involved the wearing of armbands by students), the Court's decision provided the public school community with a clear message that a student has the right of political freedom of expression.

Tinker v. Des Moines Indep. Community Sch. Dist.
393 U.S. 503, 89 S. Ct. 733, 21 L. Ed. 2d 731 (1969)

Topic: Freedom of Expression

Facts: School authorities had adopted a policy or regulation that any student wearing an armband to school would be asked to remove it and, if the student refused, he would be suspended until he returned without the armband. Three public school students wore black armbands to their schools to publicize their objections to the hostilities in Vietnam and their support for a truce. The students were suspended.

Issue: Whether the wearing of armbands is a right protected under the Free Speech Clause of the First Amendment.

Holding: Yes, the wearing of armbands is not a disruptive conduct; it is closely akin to "pure speech," which is entitled to comprehensive protection under the First Amendment. *See Tinker*, 393 U.S. at 505–06.

Reasoning:

Major Premise: The freedom of expression guaranteed by the First Amendment will apply unless it can be shown that the prohibited conduct would substantially interfere with the requirements of appropriate discipline in the operation of the school.

Minor Premise: Wearing of armbands for the purpose of expressing certain views is the type of symbolic act protected by the Free Speech Clause of the First Amendment.

Conclusion: The wearing of armbands would not interfere with the work of the school. *See Tinker*, 393 U.S. at 509.

Notes

It should be noted that the freedom of expression protected in **Tinker** pertains only to the expression of social, political, and economic issues by high school and junior high school students. Not protected is such student conduct as insolence, disrespect, obscenities, or cursing at staff members or classmates.

According to **Tinker**, "undifferentiated fear or apprehension of disturbance is not enough to overcome the right of freedom of expression." And school authorities must accept "mere disturbance" when students exercise their First Amendment rights. Only when students engage in conduct that would "materially and substantially interfere with the requirements of appropriate discipline in the operation of the school" may authorities prohibit the conduct.

A school system's policy requiring students to engage in sixty hours of community service as a condition of graduation was challenged on the grounds that it compelled expression that was protected by the First Amendment. In rejecting this claim, a federal appellate court contended that participation in the program did not affirm a belief in the philosophy of altruism on the part of participating students. See *Steirer v. Bethlehem Area School District*, 987 F.2d 989 (3rd Cir. 1993), *cert. denied* 510 U.S. 834 (1993).

A policy prohibiting the wearing or display of any gang symbol, any act or speech showing gang affiliation, and any conduct in furtherance of gang activity was upheld by a federal district court. The court related that, in this instance, the wearing of earrings by males generally connoted gang membership and did not have First Amendment protection. An equal protection argument was rejected by the court's stating "while girls may be gang members they symbolize their affiliation in other ways that are also prohibited by school policy." See *Olesen v. Board of Education*, 676 F.Supp. 820 (Ill. 1987).

Students attending private schools do not have the First Amendment protections provided by the **Tinker** decision, nor do such students necessarily have all of the civil rights guaranteed by other amendments through the Fourteenth Amendment. As mentioned earlier, however, it is prudent on the part of nonpublic school officials to at least grant a modicum of these rights. Disagreements over student rights in nonpublic schools are generally resolved by applying contract law to the situation.

B. Limiting the Tinker Doctrine

The Supreme Court decisions, such as **Bethel School District No. 403 v. Fraser** and **Hazelwood School District v. Kuhlmeier**, in the late 1980s, have tended to limit what many observers heretofore thought the **Tinker** decision allowed.

1. Nonpolitical Speech

Bethel Sch. Dist. v. Fraser
478 U.S. 675, 106 S. Ct. 3159, 92 L. Ed. 2d 549 (1986)

Topic: Freedom of Expression; Nonpolitical Speech

Facts: A high school student gave a nomination speech referring to his candidate in terms of an elaborate, graphic, and explicit sexual metaphor. The student, Matthew Fraser, was suspended for two days because the speech was considered a violation of a school rule prohibiting the use of obscene, profane language or gestures.

Issue: Whether the First Amendment's guarantee of wide freedom in matters of adult public discourse allows the same latitude to children in public school.

Holding: No, a high school student's freedom of speech right was not violated when school officials suspended him for 2 days for making sexually suggestive speech at a school assembly. The penalties imposed were unrelated to any political viewpoint, and the First Amendment did not prevent school officials from determining that to permit such lewd speech would undermine the school's basic educational mission. *See Fraser*, 478 U.S. at 685.

Reasoning:

Major Premise: The Constitution does not prohibit the states from insisting that certain modes of expression are inappropriate and subject to sanctions.

Minor Premise: The public school determined that obscene, profane language and gestures undermine the school's basic educational mission.

Conclusion: The school's rule prohibiting the use of obscene, profane language or gestures does not violate the First Amendment of the Constitution.

2. School-Sponsored Expressive Activities

Student publications and other school-sponsored expressive activities are another widely litigated freedom-of-expression issue. In many jurisdictions school newspapers were considered to be public forums, immune from attempts to regulate the viewpoints expressed therein. Student writing that was sexually suggestive, that advocated drug use, or that was potentially libelous seemingly enjoyed constitutional protection. Thus many school authorities saw their only options as either allowing the publication of such material or ceasing altogether to publish student newspapers. Against this background, the United States Supreme Court's five-to-three decision in **Hazelwood School District v. Kuhlmeier**, which addressed a school principal's censorship of student news articles, has enormous significance.

Hazelwood Sch. Dist. v. Kuhlmeier
484 U.S. 260, 108 S. Ct. 562, 98 L. Ed. 2d 592 (1988)

Topic: School Censorship of High School Newspaper

Facts: A Missouri high school newspaper was written and edited by a journalism class as part of the school's curriculum. Each issue had to be reviewed by the school principal prior to publication. On one article scheduled to appear in a coming edition, the principal objected to a pregnancy story on the grounds that the article did not adequately protect the characters' anonymity. In addition, the article's references to sexual activity and birth control were inappropriate for some younger students at the school. The principal also objected to a divorce story because the parents mentioned in the article were not given an opportunity to respond, and consent, to the article.

Issue: Whether educators may exercise control over the contents of a high school newspaper produced as part of the school's journalism curriculum, consistent with First Amendment of the Constitution.

Holding: Yes, "[E]ducators do not offend the First Amendment by exercising editorial control over the style and content of student speech in school-sponsored expressive activities so long as their actions are reasonably related to legitimate pedagogical concerns." *Hazelwood*, 484 U.S. at 273.

Reasoning:

Major Premise: The First Amendment guarantees freedom of expression in a public forum.

Minor Premise: The high school newspaper, in this case, was not opened for indiscriminate use by the general public.

Conclusion: Because the student newspaper was not a public forum, the school principal may exercise editorial control over the publication consistent with the First Amendment.

3. Use of Pagers and Cellular Phones

The use of pagers and cellular phones by public school students has increased in frequency and popularity over the past several years. Students find these devices to be affordable and convenient sources of communication both on and off school premises. Although no legal challenge has reached the courts regarding the school district's authority to restrict or prohibit their use, the courts would likely support school officials' decisions to do so unless there is evidence that a First Amendment right is in jeopardy, which is unlikely.

It is well established that school authorities may prohibit any practice that creates material or substantial disruption to the educational process. School districts may minimize legal challenges where there is evidence that the use of pagers and cellular phones creates disruption or that they are used for improper purposes. School officials are given the authority to maintain a safe and orderly environment to facilitate teaching and learning. Consequently, they may prohibit any practice that affects proper order and decorum because learning cannot occur in a disruptive environment. When school officials provide evidence that pagers and cellular phones create a disruptive influence in the school and are abused by students, they will likely succeed in prohibiting student possession of these devices on school premises while not offending the personal rights of students.

However, school boards, through district policy, may allow special exceptions in cases where such devices are needed for medical emergencies involving students with chronic illnesses or other special circumstances that warrant their use. Such exceptions should be reflected in the school district policies and require proper documentation by parents or medical experts.

C. Participation in Patriotic Exercises

Sherman v. Community School District 21 upheld a student's position not to participate in the pledge of allegiance and follows the rationale of other courts that have addressed this issue.

Sherman v. Community Sch. Dist. 21
980 F.2d 437 (7th Cir. 1991)

Topic: Participation in a Patriotic Exercise

Facts: An Illinois statute called for the daily recitation of the Pledge of Allegiance. The statute states that "The Pledge of Allegiance shall be recited each school day by pupils in elementary educational institutions supported or maintained in whole or in part by public funds." However, the law does not specify who must recite the Pledge: Some pupils? Willing pupils? Or all pupils?

Issue: Whether the daily recitation of the Pledge is coercive and in violation of the First Amendment's free speech and free exercise clauses.

Holding: No, the schools may lead the daily recitation of the Pledge of Allegiance, so long as pupils are free not to participate. *See Sherman*, 980 F.2d at 439.

Reasoning:

Major Premise: Coerced readings of the Pledge of Allegiance would pose difficulties under the free speech and free exercise clauses of the First Amendment.

Minor Premise: Because the statute is silent regarding who is required to participate in the pledge, the Court concluded that it made more sense to interpolate "by willing pupils" than "by all pupils." *See Sherman*, 980 F.2d at 442.

Conclusion: The Illinois statute does not violate the First Amendment so long as pupils are free not to participate in the Pledge.

Notes and Questions

In an earlier 1978 decision, a student's position was upheld in a refusal to stand at respectful attention during the salute to the flag. The student in this case contended that the words of the pledge were not true. See *Lipp v. Morris*, 579 F.2d 834, (3rd Cir. 1978). A student's position was also upheld in a refusal to stand during the pledge because he believed "that there (isn't) liberty and justice for all in the United States." The court did not agree that the option of either leaving the room or standing quietly during the pledge ceremony was a viable option. See *Goetz v. Ansell*, 477 F.2d 636 (2nd Cir. 1973). The United States Supreme Court upheld the rights of Jehovah's Witnesses not to participate in the pledging of the flag. See *West Virginia State Board of Education v. Barnette*, 319 U.S. 624 (1943).

Disrespect, such as burning the American flag, has been the subject of political, statutory, and judicial debate. Following the United States Supreme Court decision in *Texas v. Johnson*, 491 U.S. 397 (1989), which held a Texas law criminalizing desecration of the flag as unconstitutional, Congress enacted the Flag Protection Act of 1989, which made it a crime for anyone who "knowingly mutilates, desecrates, physically defiles, burns, maintains on the floor or ground, or tramples upon" a United States flag. In a five-to-four decision invalidating this act, the Court stated: "While flag desecration—like virulent ethnic and religious epithets, vulgar repudiations of the draft, and scurrilous caricatures—is deeply offensive to many, the Government may not prohibit the expression of an idea simply because society find the idea itself offensive or disagreeable." See *United States v. Eichman*, 496 U.S. 310 (1990).

II. SUSPENSION, EXPULSION, AND DISCIPLINARY TRANSFER

Students may be excluded from school for failure to conform to legitimate rules. Court opinions have held that since students have a valuable property interest in attending school, they must be provided due process prior to their being excluded from school. Non-disabled students may also be transferred, for disciplinary reasons, to another school from the one they are attending. Again, they must be accorded due process.

A. Suspension

Goss v. Lopez
419 U.S. 565, 95 S. Ct. 729, 42 L. Ed. 2d 725 (1975)

Topic: Suspension

Facts: An Ohio statute empowers the principal of a public school to suspend a pupil for misconduct for up to ten days. In the event of a suspension, the principal is required to notify the student's parents within 24 hours and the reasons for his action must be stated. A group of students filed suit against the Board of Education claiming that they had been suspended without a hearing, thus violating their constitutional rights.

Issue: Whether suspension from school without a hearing was in violation of the student's Fourteenth Amendment right of procedural due process.

Holding: Yes, at the very minimum, students facing a suspension must be given some kind of notice and afforded some kind of hearing. *See Goss*, 419 U.S. at 579.

Reasoning:

Major Premise: At a minimum, the Due Process Clause requires that deprivation of life, liberty, or property be preceded by notice and opportunity for hearing appropriate to the nature of the case.

Minor Premise: A student's legitimate entitlement to a public education is a property interest protected by the Due Process Clause.

Conclusion: A student's entitlement to a public education may not be taken away, by suspension, for misconduct without the minimum procedural requirement of notice and hearing.

B. Expulsion

1. Public School Expulsion

Gonzales v. McEuen
435 F.Supp. 460 (C.D. Cal. 1977)

Topic: Public School Expulsion

Facts: High school students were expelled from their high school after being charged with having committed certain acts, which, it was alleged, led to a riot at Oxnard High School. Prior to the expulsion, letters were sent to the student's parents advising them that the principal was recommending expulsion of the students. Expulsion hearings were conducted by the Board of Trustees, and the Board sustained the charges against all students and found that there was just cause for expulsion.

Issue: Whether the expulsion hearings satisfied the Fourteenth Amendment procedural due process rights of the students.

Holding: The notice given was inadequate to satisfy the Due Process Clause. Where the student is faced with the severe penalty of expulsion, the notice must communicate to the recipient (1) the nature of the proceeding; (2) a statement of the specific charge; (3) right to be represented by counsel; (4) right to present evidence; and (5) right to confront and cross-examine adverse witnesses. *See Gonzales*, 435 F.Supp. at 467.

Reasoning:

Major Premise: The requirements of due process are flexible, and different cases may require different procedural safeguards. If the possible penalties are mild, informal procedures may be sufficient. More formal proceedings may be required where severe penalties may attach.

Minor Premise: It is clear that expulsion is by far the most severe.

Conclusion: Formal proceedings are required. The notices given to the students and their parents concerning the expulsion proceedings were constitutionally inadequate and denied the student's due process rights as required by the Fourteenth Amendment.

2. Private School Expulsion

Contract law rather that constitutional law generally prevails in the expulsion of a student from a private or non-public school. Unless a substantial linkage exists between a private school and the state or federal government, the due process rights do not apply.

Allen v. Casper
622 N.E.2d 367 (Ohio Ct. App. 1993)

Topic: Private School Expulsion

Facts: Bethlehem Christian School, a privately operated institution, expelled the Allen's children on the grounds that the Allens failed to comply with admission policies and the terms of the school handbook. The dispute arose as a result of incidents that occurred at the school. Prior to the admission of their children, the Allens signed a parents' agreement and were sent a copy of the school handbook, which related to disciplinary procedures and parental involvement.

Issue: Whether the school clearly abused its discretion in enforcing its policies and regulations.

Holding: No, the relationship between the Allens and the school is a contractual one, and the terms of the relationship may be expressed by school policies and handbooks. *See Allen*, 622 N.E.2d at 371. These expressed terms may govern the circumstances under which a student may be expelled. *Id*.

Reasoning:

Major Premise: Contract law, not constitutional law, generally governs the issue of expulsion from a private school. Absent clear abuse of discretion by the school in enforcement of its policies and regulations, the court will not interfere.

Minor Premise: The Allens refused to follow the standards and procedures set forth in the handbook.

Conclusion: Officials of the Bethlehem Christian School acted within their proper discretion in removing the Allen's children.

C. Disciplinary Transfer

Transferring a student with a disability to an "alternative school," designed to meet the needs of disruptive students, is not considered to be the equivalent of an expulsion. Appropriate due process is such an instance includes: (1)

written notice to both the student and his or her parents; (2) an opportunity for a meeting among school authorities, parents, and the student, at which the situation may be discussed; and (3) a meeting at which evidence may be presented and witnesses examined. See *Jordan v. School District of City of Erie,* 583 F.2d 91 (3d Cir. 1978), and *Zamora v. Pomerroy,* 639 F.2d 662 (10th Cir. 1981).

D. Zero Tolerance and School Safety

After Columbine and other similar incidents, school safety has become a leading priority for school leaders across the nation. Many districts have initiated a zero tolerance policy in an effort to reduce school violence. Opponents are raising questions as to whether school leaders are going too far and moving too swiftly with a "one strike, and you're out" approach and whether students' First and Fourteenth Amendment rights are being jeopardized.

In 1994, the Gun Free School Act was passed. This federal statute affects each state that receives federal funds and requires local educational agencies to expel from school for a period of not less than one year any student who is found to have brought a weapon to school. Even though this statute is a version of the zero tolerance policy, it does provide flexibility based on administrative discretion. Thus, in the strictest sense, it is not absolute zero tolerance. In contrast, a recent controversy in Decatur, Illinois is an example of zero tolerance that failed to provide administrative discretion. Seven students involved in a brawl at a football game in which no weapons were involved and no serious injuries occurred were expelled for two years based on the district's zero tolerance policy. Their expulsions were later reduced to one year as a result of strong protests from segments of the community. Critics expressed concern that the penalty was unduly harsh and not proportional to the offense. Because of the escalating controversy, and to avoid legal complications, the Governor bent the rules to allow these students to attend an alternative school.

Since zero tolerance has emerged in a number of districts, students have been affected in ways that raise questions regarding the legal defensibility of these approaches. For example, a 16-year-old female student in Washington was met by police and expelled for using her finger to make a gun and jokingly saying, "Bang." She has since been reinstated. A 13-year-old male student in Texas was arrested and spent five days in jail awaiting a hearing for writing a spooky story about killing classmates. He is currently receiving home schooling. An 18-year-old male student in Georgia wrote a story in his journal about a deranged student who goes on a rampage at school, which resulted in expulsion and arrest with no opportunity to graduate. Other accounts involve a 7-year-old who was suspended for bringing nail clippers to school in Illinois and a 15-year-old in Virginia for dying his hair blue.

As school officials move toward implementing zero tolerance, they are expected to do so in a way that would ensure that their approach is legally defensible and does not violate the principles of the First and Fourteenth Amendments. Policies that do not weigh the severity of the offense, the student's history of past behavior, due process, and alternative education for students involved in long-term expulsion are, at best, highly risky. School officials are expected to strike a delicate balance between providing a safe place for their students and teachers and supporting the liberty and due process rights of the students under their care.

III. CORPORAL PUNISHMENT

Corporal punishment is the use of physical force, such as spanking, striking, and paddling. Proponents of corporal punishment view it as necessary to a maintain order in the classroom. Those opposed view it as cruel and barbaric. The issue had been repeatedly litigated until the Supreme Court upheld the practice in **Ingraham v. Wright.** In its decision, the Court addressed two major issues: whether prior notice and an opportunity to be heard were required; and whether corporal punishment amounted to cruel and unusual punishment under the Eighth Amendment.

Ingraham v. Wright
430 U.S. 651, 97 S. Ct. 1401, 51 L. Ed. 2d 711 (1977)

Topic: Corporal Punishment

Facts: In the 1970–1971 school year, many of the 237 schools in Dade County used corporal punishment as a means of maintaining discipline. The local school board, pursuant to Florida legislation, authorized punishment consisting of paddling the recalcitrant student on the buttocks with a flat wooden paddle. Normal punishment was limited to one to five "licks" or blows with the paddle and resulted in no apparent physical injury to the student. Ingraham, a pupil in a Dade County, Florida, junior high school was subjected to more than 20 licks with a paddle because he was slow to respond to his teacher's instructions. He suffered hematoma requiring medical attention and keeping him out of school for several days.

Issues: Whether the paddling of students as a means of maintaining school discipline constitutes cruel and unusual punishment in violation of the Eighth Amendment. Whether the Due Process Clause of the Fourteenth Amendment requires prior notice and an opportunity to be heard.

Holding: The Eighth Amendment, designed to protect those convicted of crime, does not apply to disciplinary paddling of public school students. *See Ingraham*, 430 U.S. at 664. The Due Process Clause of the Fourteenth Amendment does not require notice and a hearing prior to the imposition of corporal punishment in the public schools. *See id*. at 676. The common law allows teachers to inflict reasonable corporal punishment on children in their care, and it also provides civil and criminal sanctions in cases of abuse. *See id*. at 674–78.

Reasoning:

Major Premise: The Eighth Amendment is directed at the method or kind of punishment imposed for violation of a criminal statute. Where school authorities, acting under color of state law, deliberately punish a child and inflict appreciable physical pain, the Fourteenth Amendment liberty interests are implicated. *See Ingraham*, 430 U.S. at 674.

Minor Premise: The prisoner and the school children stand in wholly different circumstances, separated by the harsh facts of criminal conviction and incarceration. *See* 430 U.S. at 669. The limits of the common-law privilege, and the openness of the school environment, afford adequate protection to the child's due process rights. *See id*. at 676–77.

Conclusion: The Eighth Amendment does not apply to disciplinary paddling of schoolchildren. The Fourteenth Amendment does not require notice and hearing prior to the imposition of corporal punishment.

Notes and Questions

According to **Ingraham**, in the absence of legislation to the contrary, teachers may inflict corporal punishment. Almost half of the states do not allow the practice of corporal punishment. This is a rare instance in which a state law can take precedence over constitutional law. This is only the case because the Court declared that corporal punishment be used only "in the absence of legislation to the contrary." Even in states that allow corporal punishment, excessive punishment can be litigated under the definition of "assault and battery." A word to the wise is to avoid the use of corporal punishment even if one's school district allows it. There are many alternative ways of disciplining children that are not nearly as risky to either the child or the teacher.

IV. SEARCH OF STUDENTS AND LOCKERS

The Fourth Amendment was included in the Bill of Rights to protect the individual from possible harassment by an unresponsive government. School officials may be placed in the position of searching a student because they have a reasonable suspicion that the student has stolen an article or money or has something illegal in his or her possession, such as drugs. Courts faced with such questions have had to balance an individual student's right to the Fourth Amendment's protection from unreasonable search against the duty of school officials to provide all students with a safe and secure environment.

Another question is the degree of suspicion a school official must have before a search may be conducted. Police must have probable cause to search someone. This is a higher standard than reasonable suspicion, which has been required by those courts upholding searches by school officials. Also, courts have made a distinction when a search involves any indignities toward students, such as a stripe search or urinalysis. Such searches, according to several courts, require a standard higher than reasonable suspicion and, depending on the severity of the intrusion on the student, may require probable cause.

A. Student Search

New Jersey v. T. L. O.
469 U.S. 325, 105 S. Ct. 733, 83 L. Ed. 2d 720 (1985)

Topic: Search and Seizure in Public Schools

Facts: A teacher, upon discovering two students smoking cigarettes in the school lavatory, took them to the principal's office. After denying that she had been smoking, the principal opened T.L.O.'s purse and found a pack of cigarettes and a package of rolling papers commonly associated with marijuana use. The principal then proceeded to conduct a thorough search of the purse and found some marijuana, a pipe, plastic bags, a substantial amount of money, and two letters implicating the student in marijuana dealing.

Issue: Whether the search by the school principal violated the Fourth Amendment's prohibition against unreasonable search and seizure.

Holding: No, the Fourth Amendment prohibition of unreasonable search and seizures applies to searches conducted by public school officials. In addition, the legality of a search of a student should depend simply on the reasonableness, under all circumstances, of the search. *See T.L.O.*, 469 U.S. at 341. In this case, the Court found that the search was reasonable.

Reasoning:

Major Premise: Ordinarily, a search under the Fourth Amendment must be based on probable cause to believe that a violation of law has occurred.

Minor Premise: The Court has, in a number of cases, recognized the legality of searches and seizures based on suspicions that, although "reasonable," do not rise to the level of probable cause.

Conclusion: The search by the school official was reasonable, under the circumstances because (1) the search by the principal was justified based on a reasonable suspicion that the search will turn up evidence that the student has violated or is violating either the law or the rules of the school; and (2) the search was reasonably related to its objective and not extremely intrusive in light of the age and sex of the student and the nature of the infraction. *See* 469 U.S. at 341–42.

B. Intrusive Search

Bellnier v. Lund
438 F. Supp. 47 (N.D.N.Y. 1977)

Topic: Intrusive Search of a Student's Person

Facts: A fifth-grade student, Leonti, complained to a student teacher, Olson, that he was missing $3 from his coat pocket. The classroom teacher, Reardon, made an appeal to the class regarding knowledge of the missing money. The appeal proved fruitless. Being aware of prior complaints from class members of missing money, lunches, and other items, and knowing that no one had left the classroom, Reardon and other school officials commenced a search of the whole class. Initially, they searched the outer garments hanging in the coatroom. Then the students were asked to empty their pockets and remove their shoes. The class members were then taken to their respective bathrooms and ordered to strip down to their undergarments, and their clothes were searched. Finally, a search was conducted of the student's desks, books, and once again their coats. Despite a search that lasted approximately two hours, the missing money was never located.

Issue: Whether the search conducted by school officials violated the student's rights under the Fourth Amendment's proscription against unreasonable search and seizure.

Holding: Yes, to be a reasonable search, the Fourth Amendment requires, at a minimum, that public school officials must be able to point to particularized facts with respect to which pupil might have possessed the allegedly stolen $3 before a search can be conducted. Factors to be considered are the child's age, child's history and record in school, seriousness and prevalence of the problem to which the search is directed, and the exigency requiring immediate warrantless search. *See Bellnier*, 438 F. Supp. at 53.

Reasoning:

Major Premise: Fourth Amendment, as applied to searches conducted by school officials, requires a lesser standard than probable cause to determine the reasonableness of the search.

Minor Premise: In determining the reasonableness of the search of students, school officials must be able to point to specific facts with respect to which students might have possessed the allegedly stolen money.

Conclusion: Based on the facts, it is entirely possible that there was reasonable suspicion, and even probable cause, to believe that someone in the classroom has possession of the money. However, there were no specific facts that would allow the school officials to particularize with respect to which students might have possessed the allegedly stolen money.

C. Search for Drugs

Ordinarily, federal courts of appeals have not tended to allow strip searches. However, a strip search of a sixteen-year-old student in a behavioral disorder program who was suspected of storing drugs in his crotch area was held to be reasonable. The court contended that there were several factors influencing the decision. These included allegations of several recent prior incidents, such as dealing in drugs, testing positive for marijuana, possession of drugs, having "crotched" drugs during a police raid at his mother's house, failing a urine analysis for cocaine, unsuccessful completion of a drug rehabilitation program, and a report by a bus driver that there was a smell of marijuana where the student had sat on the bus. See *Cornfield v. Consolidated High School District No. 230*, 991 E.2d 1316 (7the Cir. 1993).

Although drugs were ultimately found in a student's car, the search in a Texas case was held to be unreasonable. In this instance, the student was patted down while attempting to determine whether he was attempting to skip school. Nothing was found. Subsequently, the student's clothing and person, locker, and car were searched. The court contended that even in light of receiving information a week earlier that the student was selling drugs, his attempting to skip school and the initial pat-down not revealing any contraband did not justify the subsequent searches. See *Coronado v. State*, 835 S.W.2d 636 (Tex. Ct. App. 1992).

Drug-searching dogs are sometimes used to identify the students who should be strip searched. A federal appellate court has held that sniffing by a dog was not a search and therefore not protected by the Fourth Amendment; requesting students to empty their pockets and purses did not violate the Fourth Amendment; but conducting a strip search of a student as a result of the dog's alert was unreasonable. In entitling the student to damages, the court contended that a strip search was not only unconstitutional but also contrary to common decency. See *Doe v. Renfrow*, 635 F.2d 582 (7th Cir. 1980), *cert. denied*, 463 U.S. 1207 (1983).

Vernonia Sch. Dist. v. Acton
515 U.S. 646, 115 S. Ct. 2386, 132 L. Ed. 2d 564 (1995)

Topic: Drug Testing of School Athletes.

Facts: Teachers and administrators in an Oregon public school district observed a sharp increase in student drug use and disciplinary problems. After discovering that athletes were leaders in the student drug culture and concern that drug use increases the risk of sports-related injury, the school district adopted the Student Athlete Drug Policy. The policy authorizes random urinalysis drug testing for students participating in their school's athletic program.

A seventh-grade student was denied participation in the school's football program because the student and his parents refused to sign the testing consent forms. A suit was filed against the school district on the grounds that the drug testing policy violated the Federal Constitution's Fourth Amendment proscription against unreasonable searches.

Issue: Whether random urinalysis drug testing of student athletes violates the Fourth Amendment's prohibition against unreasonable searches.

Holding: No, the Court applied a three-factor test: (1) "the nature of the privacy interest upon which the search here at issue intrudes." 132 L. Ed. 2d at 575; (2) "the character of the intrusion that is complained of." *Id*. at 577; and (3) "the nature and immediacy of the governmental concern at issue here, and the efficacy of the means for meeting it." *Id*. at 579.

The Student Athlete Drug Policy was reasonable under the circumstances considering (1) the student athlete's decreased expectation of privacy; (2) the relative unobtrusiveness of the search; and (3) the severity of the need met by the search. *See Vernonia*, 132 L. Ed. 2d at 582.

Reasoning:

Major Premise: Under the Fourth Amendment, the ultimate measure of the constitutionality of a governmental search is "reasonableness." 132 L. Ed. 2d at 574.

Minor Premise: Whether a particular search meets the reasonableness standard is judged by balancing its intrusion on the individual's Fourth Amendment interests against its promotion of legitimate governmental interests. *Id*.

Conclusion: After considering all the factors—the decreased expectation of privacy, the relative unobtrusiveness of the search, and the severity of the need met by the search—Vernonia's Policy is reasonable and hence constitutional.

Trinidad Sch. Dist. No. 1 v. Lopez
No. 97SC124, 1998 WL 373305, at *1 (Colo. June 29, 1998)

Topic: Drug Testing of Students Participating in Extracurricular Activities.

Facts: The school district adopted a policy, entitled "Drug Testing Student Athletes/Cheerleaders/Extra Curricular," mandating suspicionless urinalysis drug testing of all sixth- through twelfth-grade students participating in extracurricular activities.

Carlos Lopez, a senior high school student, was enrolled in two for-credit band classes and participated in the Trinidad High School marching band. He refused to consent to the mandatory drug testing. By and through his parents, Carlos filed a complaint alleging that the school drug policy violated his rights to be free from unreasonable searches and seizures as guaranteed by the Fourth Amendment to the United States Constitution.

Issue: Whether the school's drug policy, by mandating suspicionless urinalysis drug testing of all sixth- through twelfth-grade students participating in extracurricular activities, violated the student's rights to be free from unreasonable searches and seizures as guaranteed by the Fourth Amendment of the United States Constitution.

Holding: Yes, the school's mandatory drug testing policy was unreasonable and violates the Fourth Amendment of the United States Constitution because it failed *Vernonia*'s three-factor test. *See Lopez*, 1998 WL 373305, at *14.

The mandatory drug policy is unreasonable because (1) the nature of the privacy interest of students participating in extracurricular activities is different from that of the student athletes described by the *Vernonia* Court; (2) although the District established that it has a drug abuse problem, the means chosen to deal with this problem was too broad. *Id.*

Reasoning:

Major Premise: In *Vernonia*, the Supreme Court established the framework for analyzing the constitutionality of a public school district's drug testing program. *Id.* at *9. The *Vernonia* Court applied a three-factor test: (1) "the nature of the privacy interest upon which the search here at issue intrudes," (2) "the character of the intrusion that is complained of," and (3) "the nature and immediacy of the governmental concern at issue here, and the efficacy of the means for meeting it." Id. at *10.

Minor Premise: In *Lopez*, there is a significant absence of both true voluntariness and the type of communal undressing that occurred among student athletes in *Vernonia*. *Id.* at *14. In addition, the drug policy extended vastly beyond the policy upheld in *Vernonia. Id.* "The Policy swept within its reach students participating in an extracurricular activity who were not demonstrated to play a role in promoting drugs and for whom there was no demonstrated risk of physical injury." *Id.*

Conclusion: The mandatory drug policy is unconstitutional.

Notes

The Supreme Court case *Earls v. Board of Education of Tecumseh Public School District*, 122 S.Ct. 2559 (2002), was another display of the courts' favorable disposition toward drug testing. In effect, **Earls** overturned *Trinidad*. In **Earls**, an Oklahoma school policy required students participating in competitive, non-athletic extracurricular activities to be randomly tested for drugs. The court found the policy to be a reasonably effective way of addressing the school district's legitimate concerns in preventing, deterring, and detecting drug use. The school district's concern outweighed the privacy expectation of the students.

As we have seen, one of the more invasive forms of violating a person's privacy is through a strip search. In *Cornfield v. Consolidated High School District No. 230*, 991 E.2d 1316, Brian Cornfield was forced to submit to a strip search against his own will. He was suspected of storing drugs in his crotch area. When confronted about the drugs, he was outraged and refused a search. The teacher and dean made Brian strip down to his underclothes and change into gym clothes, while they watched. They found no evidence of drugs or any other contraband. In the process of deciding on this case, the court engaged in a two-pronged test to decide if the search was constitutional. First, they had to determine if the search was justified at its inception and, second, if it was permissible in scope. The measures taken to perform the search must not be excessively intrusive in light of the age and sex of the student. In this case, the court upheld the search as reasonable, therefore not violating the constitutional rights of the student. The court contended that there were several factors influencing the decision. These included allegations of recent drug incidents involving dealing drugs, testing positive for marijuana, possession of drugs, failing a urine analysis for cocaine, unsuccessful completion of drug rehabilitation programs, and being found with drugs in his crotch during a police raid. The school officials involved in the search had enough reasonable cause. The administrators had to weigh the interest of the school in maintaining order against the substantial privacy interests of students.

D. Locker Search

The courts have allowed searches of school lockers without a warrant and without the student's permission. The court's reasoning is often that schools retain ultimate control over the lockers because they own them, and they act *in loco parentis*. This issue was addressed nearly three decades ago in *Kansas v. Stein*, 203 Kan. 638, 456, P.2d 1 (1969), *cert. denied*, 397 U.S. 947 (1970), which discussed the public nature of student lockers. The court held that school authorities must protect both the school's educational functions and the students' welfare and may, therefore, inspect lockers to prevent their illicit use.

Courts have continued to uphold locker searches by school authorities, usually applying a standard that declares students to have legitimate expectations of privacy in their lockers. However, the expectation is not absolute and must be balanced against the school's need to maintain order and control.

Notes

The use of metal detectors in schools has increased over the past ten years because school violence has increased. The first case to litigate the constitutionality of metal detector searches was *People v. Dukes*. In this case, a New York school district allowed officers to use handheld metal detectors as students filed into school. If the detectors sounded twice, the officers were instructed to conduct a pat-down search. Dukes argued that the use of metal detectors was intrusive and a violation of his Fourth Amendment rights. The courts ruled that the use of hand-held detectors was considered to be unobtrusive and allowable under the Fourth Amendment.

In another case, People of the *State of Illinois v. Pruitt* argued that the use of metal detectors was a violation of their Fourth Amendment rights. The court ruled in favor of the school based upon the same rationale as in **Dukes**. The court once again stated the use of metal detectors is a reasonable search because it is virtually unobtrusive and does not invade the privacy of the student while walking through the detector.

On the other hand, not all courts agree with the previous rulings. In the case of the *Los Angeles Unified School District v. Stevens*, the court ruled in favor of the defendant Janet Stevens. While Janet was walking through the metal detector that was used by the school, the machine broke down and Janet was instructed to stay where she was until they could get the machine fixed. When the machine was fixed, the x-ray monitor revealed one of Janet's breasts and a birth control patch that she was wearing on her stomach. Other people that were in line saw the image and some students even took pictures of the image on their camera cell phones. Facing embarrassment, Janet stopped going to school and was forced to tell her father what had happened after having a meeting with the school principal regarding the excessive absences. The family sued the school district on the basis of unreasonable search and seizure. The courts ruled that the search of Janet Stevens' person exceeded the scope justified by the special needs of Belmont High School and was therefore unreasonable and illegal.

The difference between these cases was simply the type of metal detector that was used. In the cases of **Dukes** and **Pruitt**, those school districts used a detector that just alerted officials of different kinds of metals. In **Stevens**, a special x-ray machine that exposed images of student bodies under their clothes was used.

V. DRESS AND GROOMING

In the 1970s, there were many challenges to dress and grooming regulations. Students and their parents often questioned rules, particularly those pertaining to grooming, which they believed to be unfair or anachronistic. In their suits, parents commonly alleged that they, not the schools, were responsible for the appearance of their children. They contended that school authorities were warranted in imposing only those standards necessary for health, safety, or an educationally sound program. School authorities, on the other hand, usually contended that they possessed the discretion to determine which policies aided in maintaining order and discipline. Despite the controversy surrounding the issue and the judiciary's frequent involvement, the Supreme Court has not ruled on a dress and grooming case.

A. Dress

The Courts have lacked consistency in their decisions regarding the issue of dress. Generally, dress codes have been upheld that prohibited immodest or suggestive clothing, dress that would create a disturbance or distraction, and clothing that was unsanitary or created a health hazard. Because there was no showing that the wearing of blue jeans inhibited the educational process, a New Hampshire federal court, in **Bannister v. Paradis**, invalidated the prohibition against wearing jeans.

Bannister v. Paradis
316 F. Supp. 185 (D. N.H. 1970)

Topic: Dress Codes in Public School

Facts: Kevin Bannister, a sixth-grader at the Pittsfield High School, was sent home from school for violating the school's dress code prohibiting the wearing of blue jeans to school.

Issue: Whether the prohibition of wearing dungarees is a deprivation of any rights, privileges, or immunities secured by the Constitution of the United States.

Holding: Yes, a person's right to wear clothes of his own choosing provided that, in the case of a schoolboy, they are neat and clean, is a constitutional right protected and guaranteed by the Fourteenth Amendment. *See Bannister*, 316 F. Supp. at 188. The school officials have not shown that the wearing of dungarees in any way inhibited or tended to inhibit the educational process. Lacking this justification, the intrusion on the personal liberty of the student, small as the intrusion may be, is unconstitutional and invalid. *Id.* at 189.

Reasoning:

Major Premise: A school board has the power to adopt reasonable restrictions on dress as a part of its educational policy and as an educational device.

Minor Premise: School officials need to show that wearing of dungarees inhibits or tend to inhibit the educational process.

Conclusion: Since school officials were not able to show that the wearing of dungarees is a reasonable and justifiable restriction, as part of the school's educational policy, the dress code is unconstitutional.

B. Grooming

In dealing with grooming, the courts have been as inconsistent as they have been with student dress. Judicial views range from upholding the right of males to wear shoulder length hair, on the basis that this right is protected by the federal Constitution, to declaring the question an unworthy one for federal court attention.

Davenport v. Randolph County Bd. Of Educ.
730 F.2d 1395 (11th Cir. 1984)

Topic: Grooming

Facts: Randolph County High School football and basketball coach instituted a "clean shaven" policy for participating students. Two students, with parental consent, refused to abide by the policy and are suspended from the team. The student's fathers testified that they had suffered skin problems as youths caused by shaving, and that they are concern that shaving will cause their son's skin problems.

Issue: Whether the "clean shaven" policy is unconstitutional because it is arbitrary and unreasonable to require fourteen- and fifteen-year-old adolescents to shave in order to participate in high school athletics.

Holding: No, the "clean shaven" policy is within the school board's power to regulate grooming, and the students have not proven unique circumstances that would render the policy arbitrary or unreasonable. *See Davenport*, 730 F.2d at 1398.

Reasoning:

Major Premise: Grooming regulations are a reasonable means of furthering the school board's undeniable interest in teaching hygiene, instilling discipline, asserting authority, and compelling uniformity. *See* 730 F.2d at 1397.

Minor Premise: The constitutional validity of grooming policies does not apply if the policy has arbitrary effect or is unreasonable.

Conclusion: Students have not proven that unique circumstances will render the grooming policy arbitrary or unreasonable, therefore the policy is constitutionally valid.

VI. PREGNANCY, PARENTHOOD, AND MARRIAGE

The law on the issues of pregnancy, parenthood, and marriage has evolved from a time when students would be expelled in these instances, to the present time when these conditions are protected by law. Enactment of Title IX of the Education Amendments of 1972 addressed the issue on the basis of prohibiting sexual discrimination in any education programs receiving federal funds. Section 86.40, Marital or Parental Status, of the implementing regulation for Title IX states:

Marital or parental status

  (a) Status generally: A recipient shall not apply any rule concerning a student's actual or potential parental, family or marital status which treats a student differently on the basis of sex.
  (b) Pregnancy and related condition. (1) A recipient shall not discriminate against any student, or exclude any student from its education program or activity, including any class or extracurricular activity, on the basis of such student's pregnancy, childbirth, false pregnancy, termination of pregnancy or recovery therefrom, unless the student requests voluntarily to participate in a separate portion of the program or activity of the recipient.
  (c) A recipient may require such a student to obtain the certification of a physician that the student is physically and emotionally able to continue participation in the normal education program or activity so long as such a certification is required of all students for other physical or emotional conditions requiring the attention of a physician.
  (d) A recipient which operates a portion of its education program or activity separately for pregnant students, admittance to which is completely voluntary on the part of the student as provided in paragraph (b) (1) of this section shall ensure that the instructional program in the separate program is comparable to that offered to non-pregnant students.
  (e) A recipient shall treat pregnancy, childbirth, false pregnancy, termination of pregnancy and recovery therefrom in the same manner and under the same policies as any other temporary disability with respect to any medical or hospital benefit, service, plan or policy which such recipient administers, operates, offers, or participates in with respect to students admitted to the recipient's educational program or activity.
  (f) In the case of a recipient which does not maintain a leave policy for its students, or in the case of a student who does not otherwise qualify for leave under such a policy, a recipient shall treat pregnancy, childbirth, false pregnancy, termination of pregnancy and recovery therefrom as a justification for a leave of absence for so long a period of time as is deemed medically necessary by the student's physician, at the conclusion of which the student shall be reinstated to the status which she held when the leave began, 45 C.F.R. 86.40.

In an alleged Title IX violation, a federal court of appeals addressed a female student's dismissal from a chapter of the National Honor Society because of her pregnancy. In its decision, the court stated that premarital sex, rather than gender, and pregnancy or failure to marry could be reasons taken into account for the student's dismissal. Faculty members had stated that failure to uphold standards of leadership and character, not the pregnancy, were the basis for dismissal. The court also concluded that not dismissing a male member from the Society who had engaged in premarital sex was relevant in determining whether members of the faculty had a double standard and, therefore, intentionally discriminated against the pregnant student. See *Pfeiffer v. Marion Center Area School District*, 917 F.2d 779 (3rd Cor. 1990).

VII. EDUCATION OF INDIVIDUALS WITH DISABILITIES

Before relatively recently, the situation regarding students with disabilities may be characterized by a philosophy that placed the burden of educating children with disabilities primarily on the family. As a result, the severely disabled were not considered the responsibility of the public schools and were exempt from compulsory attendance laws.

The passage of state and federal laws and a series of court decisions in the 1970s dramatically altered the relationship between students with disabilities and public schools. In 1970, the Education of the Handicapped Act was passed. The passage of this legislation brought increased national attention to policy issues regarding students with disabilities. A Bureau of Education for the Handicapped was created, and, although early legislation did not provide for "mainstreaming" or a free and appropriate education, it establishes the groundwork for future legislation dealing with those issues.

Several successful court challenges to existing practices also altered the historic relationship between students with disabilities and the public schools. Two of these decisions are particularly noteworthy. A federal district court in *Pennsylvania Association for Retarded Children v. Pennsylvania*, 343 F. Supp. 279 (Pa. 1972), held that mentally retarded students between the ages of six and twenty-one should be provided with access to a free public education and that students with disabilities would be placed in regular classrooms when possible or in special classes when necessary. In *Mills v. Board of Education of the District of Columbia*, 348 F. Supp. 866 (D.C. 1972), another federal district court extended this doctrine to all school-aged children with disabilities, holding that they must be provided with a free and adequate public education.

The federal laws that followed these cases embodied many of the principles enunciated in these court decisions. Section 504 of the Rehabilitation Act of 1973, for example, represented a national commitment to end discrimination in any program receiving federal funds. The education for All Handicapped Children Act of 1975 (P.L. 94-142) heralded a national policy under which federal funds would subsidize special education in those states meeting qualification requirements. The cornerstone of this legislation required states to adopt policies that assure all "handicapped" children a "free appropriate public education." The Education for the Handicapped Act Amendments of 1990 gave the Act a new title—Individuals with Disabilities Education Act (IDEA). The language of IDEA used the term "disability" instead of "handicap" and person-first language, i.e., children with disabilities. The Americans with Disabilities Act of 1990 became effective in 1992. It extends civil rights protections to individuals with disabilities to private sector employment, in addition to public services, public accommodations, transportation, and telecommunications.

A. The Limits of "Free Appropriate Education"

The Education for All Handicapped Children Act imposed strict obligations upon participating states to meet the educational needs of children with disabilities. In the years immediately following the Act's passage, school districts claiming in court to lack the resources to implement it usually were unable to prevail on the basis of this claim. It seemed to many observers that the Act obligated schools to provide, on demand and regardless of cost, optimal educational services to meet any demonstrated educational need. Then, in 1982, the United State Supreme Court delivered a decision that addressed the limitation of the Act's guarantees.

Board of Educ. of the Hendrick Hudson Cent. Sch. Dist. v. Rowley
458 U.S. 176, 102 S. Ct. 3034, 73 L. Ed. 2d 690 (1982)

Topic: Defining the Limits of "Free Appropriate Education"

Facts: The Education of the Handicapped Act provides federal money to assist state and local agencies in educating handicapped children, and conditions such funding upon a state's compliance with extensive goals and procedures. The state must ensure all handicapped children the right to a "free appropriate public education" tailored to the unique needs of the handicapped children by means of an "individualized educational program" (IEP).

Amy Rowley is a deaf student at the Furnace Woods School in the Hendrick Hudson Central School District, Peekskill, New York. Amy has minimal residual hearing and is an excellent lip-reader. The school furnished Amy with a special hearing aid for use in the classroom and also provided her with additional instruction from tutors. Amy was advancing easily from grade to grade and she was also performing better than average children in her class. Nonetheless, her parents insisted that Amy also be provided a qualified sign-language interpreter in all her academic classes. The school denied this request and this suit followed.

Issue: Whether the requirement of "free appropriate public education" requires that the state maximize the potential of each handicapped child commensurate with the opportunity provided to non-handicapped children.

Holding: No, the "free appropriate public education" test is satisfied if personalized instruction is being provided to a handicapped child with sufficient supportive services to permit the child to benefit educationally from that instruction. *Rowley*, 458 U.S. at 188–89. Such instruction (1) must be provided at public expense; (2) must meet the state's educational standards; (3) must approximate the grade levels used in the state's regular education; and (4) must comport with the child's IEP. *Id*. at 203.

If the child is being educated in the regular classrooms of the public education system, the personalized instruction should be reasonably calculated to enable the child to achieve passing marks and advance from grade to grade. *Id*. At 204.

Reasoning:

Major Premise: Congress sought primarily to identify and evaluate handicapped children and to provide them with access to a free public education. The "basic floor of opportunity" provided by the Act consists of access to specialized instruction and related services, which are individually designed to provide educational benefit to the handicapped child. 458 U.S. at 201.

Minor Premise: Amy is receiving an "adequate" education because she performs better than the average children in her class and is advancing easily from grade to grade. *See id*. at 209. She is also "receiving personalized instruction and related services calculated by the Furnace Woods school administrators to meet her educational needs." *Id*. at 210.

Conclusion: The Act does not require the school to maximize each handicapped child's potential commensurate with the opportunity provided to other non-handicapped children. Therefore, the state is not required to provide a sign-language interpreter.

Notes

Guidelines regarding "mainstreaming" have been provided in a case of a child with Down's syndrome who was placed in a state school for the disabled, despite his parent's desire that he be placed in a regular elementary school. In upholding the school district, the court noted that the Education for All Handicapped Children Act does not absolutely require mainstreaming but rather mandates it "to the maximum extent appropriate." The court concluded that children with disabilities are not entitled to the best possible education; instead, a school district considering a disabled student's placement may weigh the benefits to the child against the costs to the district. In this case, the student was so severely disabled that his interaction with "regular" students would have been limited to observing them. See *A.W. v. Northwest R-1 School District*, 813 F.2d 158 (8th Cir. 1987), *cert. denied*, 484 U.S. 847 (1987). It is interesting, however, to find that many school districts will "mainstream" disabled students no matter how severe the disability for fear that its public image will be tarnished if they refuse such accommodation.

B. Individualized Educational Program Requirement

When the evaluation results of disabled students are produced, an individualized educational program (IEP) must be designed for each child. This process usually involves one or more meetings in which the child's teachers, parent, and a special education representative from the district are present to review and discuss evaluation results. It is also recommended that a representative from the evaluation team be present to respond to questions and interpret results. If feasible, this person may be represented by the child's teacher or the special education supervisor. At a minimum, each IEP should include the following:

1. A statement detailing the child's present level of educational performance.
2. A statement of annual goals, as well as short-term instructional objectives.
3. A description of specific educational services to be provided and a determination as to whether the child is able to participate in regular educational programs.
4. A description of transitional services to be rendered if the child is a junior or senior in high school, to ensure that necessary services are provided when the child leaves the regular school environment.
5. A description of services to be provided and a timetable for providing these services.
6. An explanation of relevant criteria and procedures to be employed annually to determine if instructional objectives are or have been achieved.

C. Equal Access to Assistive Technology for Students with Disabilities

The Technology-Related Assistance for Individuals with Disabilities Act Amendment of 1994 provides financial assistance to states to support systems changes that assist in the development and implementation of technology-related support for individuals with disabilities. The Act further ensures timely acquisition and delivery of assistive technology *devices*, including equipment and product systems commercially acquired, modified, or customized that are used to increase, maintain, or improve functional capabilities of a child with disabilities.

Technology assistive *services* are also included in this Act and involve any service that directly assists a child with a disability in the selection, acquisition, or use of an assistive technology device. These services may include (1) purchasing, leasing, or otherwise providing for the acquisition of assistive technology by the child; (2) selecting, designing, fitting, customizing, adapting, applying, maintaining, repairing, or replacing assistive technology devices; (3) coordinating and using other therapies, interventions, or service with assistive technology devices, such as those associated with existing education and rehabilitation plans and programs; (4) training or technical assistance for the child or, where appropriate, the family of such children; and (5) training or technical assistance for professionals, employers, and other individuals who provide services to, employ, or are otherwise substantially involved in the major life functions of the child.

As part of assistive technology service, training for teachers, employers, administrators, and/or any other persons who are dealing directly with student disabilities must be accommodated. Training needs may include:

1. An understanding of federal law—Section 504, ADA, and/or IDEA.
2. An understanding of their responsibilities in providing accommodations.
3. An understanding of the rights of the child with disabilities.
4. An understanding of how accommodations and modifications should be provided.

With the previous in mind, each IEP must be reviewed and revised annually, if necessary, to ensure that the continuing needs of the child are met. If changes are contemplated, the child's parent or legal guardian must be notified. If either objects to the proposed changes, an impartial hearing must be held to resolve the conflict. If this process proves unsuccessful, the parent or guardian may appeal to the state agency and subsequently to the courts if a resolution is not reached at the state level. This appeals process is designed to ensure fundamental fairness and to meet the requirements of due process, as spelled out in the Disabilities Act.

There is also an education-related service requirement in IDEA. A related service is viewed as one that must be provided to allow the child with disabilities to benefit from special education. A related service may be a single service or an entire range of services or programs needed to benefit the child. Examples of such services include, but are not limited to, transportation, medical services, counseling services, psychological services, physical therapy, speech pathology, audiology, and occupational therapy.

Litigation has challenged precisely what is considered to be a related service. A challenge was brought by a school district in the *Irving Independent School District v. Tatro* regarding the difference between a medical service and a related service. Amber Tatro, 8 years old, was born with spina bifida. Because of a bladder condition, she was unable to urinate properly. Her condition required a clean, intermittent catheterization every three or four hours to empty her bladder and to avoid injury to her kidneys. This procedure was not considered to be complex. In fact, her parents, babysitter, and teenage brother were all trained to perform this simple procedure in a matter of minutes. The record shows that Amber would soon be able to perform this procedure herself. When Amber reached school age, her parents requested that school personnel perform this procedure as needed during the school day. The district refused, arguing that this service was a medical, rather than a related service, and did not serve the purpose of diagnosis or evaluation.

The district court held for Amber by stating that the Education for All Handicapped Children Act required that such services be provided. This decision was affirmed by the Court of Appeals and granted review by the Supreme Court. The Supreme Court upheld the previous court rulings, indicating that school authorities must provide clean, intermittent catheterization to students requiring such a procedure. The Court further enumerated that there can be no question that the IDEA mandates states to provide programs for children with disabilities, which include special education and related services necessary to achieve the act's objectives. Thus, school districts are required to provide simple medical procedures under the category of related services, when such procedures do not require complex mastery and the services are necessary for the child to benefit from an appropriate special education program.

D. Least Restrictive Environment

The IDEA embraces the notion that children with disabilities be placed in educational settings that offer the least amount of restrictions, when appropriate. This view is supported by the philosophy that children with disabilities should be educated with children who are not disabled under normal classroom conditions. The primary objective is to provide children with disabilities an opportunity to interact, socialize, and learn with "regular" students, thus minimizing the tendency to become stigmatized and isolated from the school's regular population. There is also inherent value in providing non-disabled students an opportunity to increase awareness of the many challenges faced by children with disabilities and to sensitize them to their unique needs. Thus, the least-restrictive provision of the Act mandates the inclusion of students with disabilities in regular classrooms.

The interpretation of what precisely constitutes the least-restrictive environment has led to litigation. Generally, when a child with disabilities is not involved in regular classroom instruction, the district must demonstrate through the evaluation and IEP process that a segregated facility would represent a more appropriate and beneficial learning environment. Because the law indicates a strong preference for inclusion, the burden of proof rests with educators to demonstrate that their decisions are not arbitrary or capricious regarding the placement of a child with disabilities. The statute does not mandate inclusion in each case involving such a child, but it does require that inclusion be used to the fullest extent possible and as appropriate, based on the unique needs of the child with disabilities.

E. Inclusion of Children with Disabilities

The new term that has emerged when dealing with the disabled is "full inclusion" or simply "inclusion." It has replaced the term mainstreaming in the lexicon of the disabled and denotes a step beyond mainstreaming. It is based on the idea that disabled students should be placed in regular classes full time, regardless of their mental, physical, or emotional characteristics. It is controversial because what advocates see as a civil right is many times pedagogically unsound and difficult to implement.

Implicit in this concept is the notion that some educational benefit is conferred on students with disabilities when they attend public schools. A child's evaluation results, which are used to develop the IEP, would ultimately determine the nature of the placement. Because the IEP is tailored specifically to meet the needs of the child with disabilities, it must be reasonably calculated to enable the child to receive the benefit of instruction.

Under the concept of inclusion, regular classroom teachers in schools across the country are challenged to meet the needs of students with disabilities. In many instances, teachers are unprepared to do so. Because the IDEA specifies that students with disabilities be provided a free, appropriate public education in the least restrictive environment based on each student's individualized educational program, there is an affirmative obligation placed on schools to serve the needs of these students. If teachers are not prepared to meet these needs, a legal issue may emerge regarding both academic injury as well as physical injury to the student.

With increasing frequency, regular classroom teachers are called on to meet the academic needs and perform related services, such as catheterization, suctioning, and colostomy and seizure monitoring, when students with disabilities are placed in regular classrooms. If teachers are unable to perform these vital services effectively, resulting in injury to the child, liability charges may be forthcoming, depending on the nature of the injury and factors leading to such injury. Thus, not only are classroom teachers expected to meet the academic needs of children with disabilities, but they may also be expected to provide special education–related services to them.

School districts have the responsibility of ensuring that a reasonable standard of care is met when regular teachers work with students who have disabilities. This means that districts must be properly prepared to meet the diverse needs of such students, which may be accomplished through systematic and continuous training, as well as appropriately developed policies and procedures regarding the teacher's role in relation to students with disabilities. These procedures should be monitored on a systematic basis and altered as the need arises. Failure to adhere to these precautions may form the grounds for liability suits for physical injury, as well as threats of educational malpractice if parents of children with disabilities allege that academic injury resulted from the teacher's lack of skill or fidelity in performing processional duties.

F. Disciplining Students with Disabilities

The Education for All Handicapped Children Act's guarantee of a free, appropriate education has been interpreted as prohibiting the exclusion of students with disabilities when their misbehavior is a manifestation of their disability. It may be necessary, nevertheless, to change the educational placement of a disruptive or dangerous student with disabilities who requires an environment more structured than that stipulated in the current individualized education plan. Problems often arise over the dispensation of such students during the sometimes lengthy due process that the Act requires to precede a change in placement. Although the Act apparently allows short-term suspensions of such students, a "stay put" provision states that during the term of due process, the "child shall remain in the then current educational placement."

In addressing this issue, the Supreme Court has strictly construed the "stay put" provision. In *Honig v. Doe*, 484 U.S. 305 (1988), the indefinite suspension, in accordance with California's school regulations, of two disruptive students in a program for the emotionally disabled was challenged. Although it affirmed school officials' discretion to suspend such students for ten days, the Court declared that Congress intended to "strip schools of the unilateral authority they had traditionally employed to exclude disabled students, particularly emotionally disturbed, students from school." School officials who perceive the need to remove such students from school pending the outcome of placement proceedings, and who have failed to reach an accord with parents during an initial ten-day suspension, can effect a removal only by seeking injunctive relief in court. Such an injunction was granted to change an existing individual education program (IEP), pending its review, regarding an overly aggressive student classified as emotionally disturbed, learning disabled, speech disabled, and diagnosed as exhibiting psychotic disorder. He had been involved in thirty assaults on teachers, staff, and other students; had run into other classrooms; attempted to jump out of a second-story window on two occasion; had virtually destroyed a timeout room; used profanity extensively; and, on one occasion, tried to run in front of a moving car. See *Texas City Independent School District v. Jorstad*, 752 F.Supp. 231 (Tex.1990).

In *Larry P. v. Riles,* 793 f.2d 969 (9th Cir. 1984), the parents of a disabled youngster contested his labeling. The use of IQ tests for special education placement was judged to be in violation of Title VI of the Civil Rights Act as well as the Education for All Handicapped Children Act because these tests had a history of being racially biased and resulted in a disproportionate assignment of African American students to classes for the educable mentally retarded.

Discipline procedures under the IDEA may be the most confusing issue in dealing with students with disabilities. Hence, the following list of options is provided:

1. Behavior Management Strategies: A variety of behavior and conflict management strategies, including time-outs, detention, rewards, and restrictions can be used in an attempt to modify and improve student behavior. School officials can usually unilaterally implement these behavior management strategies.
2. Acquiring Parental Consent: If more serious strategies are found to be necessary, school officials may acquire parental permission for needed changes in placement or for other appropriate behavior management measures. With parental consent, IDEA limitations on disciplinary determination usually do not apply.
3. Unilateral 10-Day Removal: In serious cases, school officials may unilaterally remove a student for up to 10 days for misconduct. No services are required, and no manifestation determination is necessary.
4. Subsequent 10-Day Removals: IDEA regulations indicate that there is no limit to the number of times that a disabled student can be removed from the classroom as no single removal exceeds 10 days. However, schools must provide services to the extent necessary to allow the child to make appropriate progress toward IEP goals.
5. Long-Term Suspensions and Expulsions: If the conduct is not a manifestation of the student's disability, the student can be suspended or expelled with normal due process. However, any removal beyond 10 days that is caused by the student's disability constitutes a change in placement, triggering IDEA due process protections. Further, schools must continue to provide a FAPE to these students.
6. 45-Day Removals for Weapons or Drugs: School officials may unilaterally remove a student to an alternative educational placement for up to 45 days for possession of weapons or drugs.
7. 45-Day Removals for Endangering Safety and Welfare: School officials may ask a hearing officer to remove a potentially dangerous student to an alternative educational placement for up to 45 days by presenting evidence that maintaining the current placement places the disabled student or the regular students' safety and welfare in serious jeopardy.
8. Obtaining a Court Order: If the above options fail, the school officials may seek to obtain a court order for removal or change of placement of the student who presents a serious threat to the well-being of the members of the school community.
9. Crime Reports: School officials may report a student suspected of committing crimes to law enforcement agents, who are not bound by IDEA regulations.

G. Private School Placement of Disabled Students

If a public school system cannot provide the educational needs for a child with disabilities, parents may be reimbursed for expenditures for private special education. However, courts have had to address the issue of entitlement to reimbursement when a child is placed in a private setting during the review process of a contested individualized education program (IEP) and placed in a private school which is not approved by the state.

Florence County Sch. Dist. v. Carter
510 U.S. 7, 114 S. Ct. 361, 126 L. Ed. 2d 284 (1993)

Topic: Education of Disabled Students

Facts: The Individuals with Disabilities Education Act (IDEA) requires states to provide disabled children with a "free appropriate public education."

Shannon Carter, a student in the Florence County School District, was classified as learning disabled. In accordance with the Act, school officials met with Shannon's parents to formulate an individualized education program (IEP). Shannon's parents requested a hearing to challenge the proposed IEP's appropriateness. In the meantime, Shannon's parents enrolled her in Trident Academy, a private school specializing in educating children with disabilities. The state and local educational authorities later concluded that the IEP was adequate, and Shannon's parents filed this lawsuit claiming that the school district had breached its duty under IDEA and sought reimbursement for tuition and other costs incurred at Trident.

Issue: Whether a Court may order reimbursement for parents who unilaterally withdraw their child from a public school that provides an inappropriate education under IDEA and put the child in a private school that provides an education that is otherwise proper under IDEA, but does not meet all of its requirements.

Holding: Yes, parents are entitled to reimbursement only if a federal court concludes that the public placement violated IDEA and that the private school placement was proper under the Act. *Carter*, 510 U.S. at 15.

Reasoning:

Major Premise: Congress meant to include retroactive reimbursement to parents as an available remedy in cases where the school district's proposed IEP was inappropriate under IDEA. 510 U.S. at 12.

Minor Premise: Public school authorities who want to avoid reimbursing parents for the private education of a disabled child can do one of two things: (1) give the child a free appropriate public education in a public setting; or (2) place the child in an appropriate private setting of the state's choice. *Id*. at 15.

Conclusion: Because the school district's public placement violated the IDEA, the Court is authorized to fashion equitable relief, such as the appropriate level of reimbursement that should be required. *Id*. at 15–16.

Notes

Two important aspects of the **Florence** case were that the public school's proposed program was inadequate, and that the private school's program was appropriate. If dissatisfied with their child's individual education program, parents should not expect reimbursement if either of these elements is missing.

In a decision dealing with the refusal of a school district to provide a sign-language interpreter to accompany a deaf child to classes at a Roman Catholic high school, the Supreme Court held that such an involvement was not barred by the Establishment Clause. The Court contended that such a service was part of the general government program that distributes benefits *neutrally* to any child qualifying as disabled under the IDEA. See *Zobrest v. Catalina Foothills School District,* 509 U.S.1 (1993).

H. Communicable Disease as a Disability

A very topical issue is whether to allow children who have HIV or AIDS to attend regular public school classes. Many parents fear that their children could contract the disease from infected children by being bitten or transferring it through saliva, tears, or an open wound.

To date, the courts have revealed a high degree of sensitivity to students with HIV or AIDS and to their being included in the regular public school classrooms. This view is presented in **Thomas v. Atascadero Unified School District.**

Thomas v. Atascadero Unified Sch. Dist.
662 F. Supp. 376 (C.D.Cal. 1987)

Topic: Communicable Disease as a Disability

Facts: Ryan Thomas was infected with the AIDS virus as an infant as the result of a contaminated blood transfusion received at the hospital where he was being treated for complications arising out of his premature birth. He is now a five-year-old kindergarten student. On September 8, 1986, Ryan got into a skirmish with another child. Ryan bit the other child's pants leg, but no skin was broken. As a result, Ryan was excluded from his kindergarten class.

Issue: Whether the exclusion from school of a child with AIDS, although consistent with the school district's reliance on guidelines and recommendations concerning the school placement of students with AIDS, is violative of the Rehabilitation Act of 1973.

Holding: Yes, a child with Acquired Immune Deficiency Syndrome (AIDS) is a "handicapped person" within the meaning of §504 of the Federal Rehabilitation Act of 1973. Under the Act, a child infected with AIDS is "otherwise qualified" to attend regular kindergarten where there is no evidence that the child poses a significant risk of harm to his kindergarten classmates or teachers. There is no evidence that Ryan Thomas poses a significant risk of harm to his kindergarten classmates or teachers; therefore, Ryan may not be excluded from attending his kindergarten class.

Reasoning:

Major Premise: A child with AIDS is protected by the Federal Rehabilitation Act of 1973, and he is "otherwise qualified" to attend school where there is no evidence that he poses a significant risk of harm to his classmates or teachers.

Minor Premise: The overwhelming weight of medical evidence is that the AIDS virus is not transmitted by human bites, even bites that break the skin. *Thomas*, 662 F. Supp. At 380. There are no reported cases of the transmission of the AIDS virus in a school setting. *Id.*

Conclusion: There is no evidence that Ryan Thomas poses a significant risk of harm to his kindergarten classmates or teachers. Therefore, he may not be excluded from attending his kindergarten class. *See id.* at 382. Ryan is "otherwise qualified" to attend a regular kindergarten class within the meaning of §504 of the Rehabilitation Act of 1973. *Id.* at 381.

I. Attention Deficit Hyperactivity Disorder

A growing number of children with attention deficit hyperactivity disorder (ADHD) are enrolled in public schools. Three federal statutes—the Individuals with Disabilities Education Act, Section 504 of the Rehabilitation Act of 1973, and the Americans with Disabilities Act—cover children with attention deficit hyperactivity disorder.

Under IDEA, ADHD eligible students must possess one or more specified physical or mental impairments and must be determined to require special education and related services based on these impairments. ADHD alone is not sufficient to qualify a child for special education services unless it impairs the child's ability to benefit from education. Children with ADHD may be eligible for special education services if they are found to have a specific learning disability, be seriously emotionally disturbed, or possess other health impairments.

Section 504 provides education for children who do not fall within the disability categories covered under IDEA. This statute further requires that a free, appropriate public education be provided to each eligible child who is disabled but does not require special education, and related services under IDEA. A free, appropriate education, as defined under Section 504, includes regular or special education and related services designed to meet the individual needs of students consistent with the provisions involving evaluation, placement, and procedural safeguards. The act stipulates:

• Parents are guaranteed the right to contest the outcome of an evaluation if a local district determines that a child is not disabled under Section 504.

- The local district is required to make an individualized determination of the child's educational needs for regular or special education or related aids and services if the child is determined to be eligible under Section 504.
- Implementation of an individualized educational program is required.
- The child's education must be provided in the regular classroom unless it is shown that the education in the regular classroom with the use of supplementary aids and services cannot be achieved satisfactorily.
- Necessary adjustments must be made in the regular classroom for children who qualify under Section 504.

The education program requirements of RHA, although not as detailed, are fairly consistent with those of IDEA. The Rehabilitation Act and Americans with Disabilities are similar regarding basic provisions. RHA regulates organizations that receive federal funds, whereas ADA covers virtually all public and private schools with the exception of private religious schools. Receipt of federal finds is not associated with ADA. Although there is overlap between these two laws, the requirements are essentially the same for both. Fundamental to both laws is the requirement that children with ADHD and other disabilities not be treated differently based solely on their disability.

VIII. PARTICIPATION IN EXTRACURRICULAR ACTIVITIES

Two legal questions arise when students are excluded from extracurricular activities. One of the issues raised the question of the status of extracurricular activities as a protected property interest and the requisite due process required, if any. The other issue deals with the equal protection claim that an excluded student is the victim of a school's arbitrary classification system.

A. Legal Status of Extracurricular Activities

Goss established the concept that students have a protected property interest in education. However, courts have not agreed whether or not participation in one aspect of the educational process, such as extracurricular activities, is a constitutionally protected property interest. If such a property interest is involved, the next question would be the extent of due process that should be provided. These issues were addressed by the Nebraska Supreme Court in **Palmer v. Merluzzi.**

Palmer v. Merluzzi
868 F.2d 90 (3d Cir. 1989)

Topic: Legal Status of Extracurricular Activities

Facts: Dan Palmer was a senior at Hunterdon Central High School and a starting wide receiver on the high school's football team. In order to fill a course requirement, Dan and three other students were assigned, without faculty supervision, to the school radio station, which is located in the school premises. The next morning, beer stains and a marijuana pipe were discovered at the radio station. At an informal hearing, Dan Palmer admitted his participation in marijuana smoking and beer drinking. As a result, Dan was assigned a ten-day out-of-school suspension. In addition, a sixty-day extracurricular suspension was imposed.

Issue: Whether the 60-day athletic suspension violated Dan Palmer's equal protection and due process rights under the Fourteenth Amendment.

Holding: Participation in extracurricular activities is not a fundamental right under the Constitution. *Palmer*, 868 F.2d at 96. A student faced with athletic suspension is not entitled to more process than that required for a ten-day academic suspension. *See id*. at 95–96. Therefore, Dan Palmer's equal protection and due process rights under the Fourteenth Amendment were not violated.

Reasoning:

Major Premise: Due process is required when a student faces a ten-day academic suspension and a sixty-day athletic suspension. Participation in extracurricular activities is not a fundamental right under the Constitution.

Minor Premise: An informal hearing process would reconcile the private and governmental interests in athletic suspensions. The state has a very strong interest in preserving a drug-free school environment and in discouraging drug use by its students.

Conclusion: An informal hearing process satisfies the due process requirements of an athletic suspension. The disciplinary actions taken by the school were rationally related to a valid state interest; therefore, the "rational relationship test" is satisfied.

Notes

In *Pegram v. Nelson,* 469 F.Supp. 1134 (N.C. 1979), the court declared:

> Since there is not a property interest in each separate component of the educational process, denial of the opportunity to participate in merely one of several extracurricular activities would not give rise to a right to due process. However, total exclusion from participation in that part of the educational process designated as extracurricular activities for a lengthy period of time could, depending upon the particular circumstances, be a sufficient deprivation to implicate due process. (p. 1140)

In *Brands v. Sheldon Community School,* 671 F.Supp. 627 (Iowa), school authorities were upheld in declaring a champion high school wrestler ineligible for the state wrestling championship. The school board's decision resulted from the wrestler's participation with three other students in having multiple acts of sexual intercourse with a sixteen-year-old female student.

The courts have addressed the issue of academic requirements for participation in extracurricular activities. These requirements, often referred to as "no pass, no play" rules, generally require that a student maintain a passing grade in all academic classes in order to be eligible to participate in extracurricular activities. Courts have considered these requirements to be constitutional and not a violation of the First or Fourteenth Amendments. See *Montana v. Board of Trustees of School District No. 1,* 726 P.2d 801 (Mont. 1986); *Spring Branch Independent School District v. Stamos,* 695 S.W.2d 556 (Tex. 1985).

B. Athletics

A great number of court cases involve exclusion from participation in athletics. Those barred from participating usually cite the Fourteenth Amendment equal protection guarantees.

1. Married Students

Cases dealing with prohibition from participating in athletics often involve athletes claiming that they are being deprived of a chance to be considered for athletic college scholarships. In the case of married students, the courts have historically upheld rules barring them from participating in athletics. However, beginning the early 1970s, around the time of **Tinker**, the courts have consistently invalidated such rules.

Beeson v. Kiowa County Sch. Dist.
567 P.2d 801 (Colo. Ct. App. 1977)

Topic: Participation of Married Students in Athletic Activities

Facts: Beeson was a senior high school student, married, and a mother of a child. She wanted to participate on the girl's varsity basketball team. She was prohibited from participating in interscholastic competition because of a school board policy prohibiting married students from participating in any extracurricular activities.

The school board justifies the school policy by (1) the need to require married students to focus on their basic education and their family responsibilities; (2) the policy discouraged teenagers from marrying until after their high school education was completed; (3) the need to discourage unwanted pregnancies; (4) married students could promote a lack of discipline among the students; and (5) the liability the school district might incur if a married woman student participating in athletics suffers injury while in the process of an undetected pregnancy.

Issue: Whether a school board policy, which prohibits married students from participating in any extracurricular activities, violates the equal protection clause of the Fourteenth Amendment of the United Sates Constitution.

Holding: Yes, discouraging eligible persons from marrying obviously contravenes the declared public policy of Colorado "to promote and foster the marriage relationship." *Beeson*, 567 P.2d at 805. A school board policy that discriminates against those who exercise their right to marriage violates the equal protection clause of the Fourteenth Amendment, unless there exists a compelling state interest that justifies that discrimination. *Id*. The school board failed to show a compelling state interest sufficient to justify discriminating against married students. *See id*. at 805–806.

Reasoning:

Major Premise: The creation of a "marriage relationship" is a fundamental right. *See id*. at 805.

Minor Premise: A policy that discriminates based solely on the fact that a person is married violates the equal protection clause of the Fourteenth Amendment, unless there exists a compelling state interest that justifies such discrimination. *See id*.

Conclusion: The school board failed to show a compelling state interest that justifies discrimination against married students, therefore the policy violates the equal protection clause of the Fourteenth Amendment.

2. Female Participation

Female participation in athletics is another area of law that evolved considerably over the years. Historically, there has been *defacto* and *dejure* segregation of male and female public school students. In some school systems, especially nonpublic school systems, entire schools have been segregated on the basis of gender. More common, however, has been the separation of the sexes in certain classes and in interscholastic athletic participation. A flagrant example has been the routine assignment of girls to home economics classes and boys to "shop" courses. Opportunities for females in athletic competition were limited, and the stereotypical role for a female was often that of cheerleader.

Many female students and their parents considered such treatment, especially in the limited opportunity for athletic competition, to be in violation of the equal protection provision of the Fourteenth Amendment and a form of sex discrimination. Many courts have agreed with this contention, and although Title IX addresses this issue, litigation pertaining to female participation in athletic programs had not abated.

Section 86.41, Athletics, of the implementing regulation for Title IX reads:

Athletics
  (a) General. No person shall, on the basis of sex, be excluded from participation in, be denied the benefit of, be treated differently from one another or otherwise be discriminated against in any interscholastic, intercollegiate, club or intramural athletics offered by a recipient, and no recipient shall provide any such athletics separately on such basis.

(b) Separate teams. Notwithstanding the requirements of paragraph (a) of this section, a recipient may operate or sponsor separate teams for members of each sex where selection for such teams is based upon competitive skill or the activity involved is a contact sport. However, where a recipient operates or sponsors a team in a particular sport for members on one sex but operates or sponsors no such team for members of the other sex, and athletic opportunities for members of that sex have previously been limited, members of the excluded sex must be allowed to try out for the team offered unless the sport involved is a contact sport. For the purposes of this part, contact sports include boxing, wrestling, rugby, ice hockey, football, basketball, and other sports the purpose or major activity of which involves bodily contact.

(c) Equal opportunity. A recipient which operates or sponsors interscholastic, intercollegiate, club or intramural athletics shall provide equal athletic opportunity for members of both sexes. In determining whether equal opportunity for members of both sexes. In determining whether equal opportunities are available the Director will consider, among other factors:

 (1) Whether the selection of sports and levels of competition effectively accommodate the interests and abilities of members of both sexes;
 (2) The provision of equipment and supplies:
 (3) Scheduling of games and practice time;
 (4) Travel and per diem allowance;
 (5) Opportunity to receive coaching and academic tutoring;
 (6) Assignment and compensation of coaches and tutors;
 (7) Provision of locker room, practice and competitive facilities;
 (8) Provision of medical and training facilities and services;
 (9) Provision of housing and dining facilities and services;
(10) Publicity.

Unequal aggregate expenditures for members of each sex or unequal expenditures for male and female teams if a recipient operates or sponsors separate teams will not constitute noncompliance with this section, but the Director may consider the failure to provide necessary funds for teams for one sex in assessing equality of opportunity for members of each sex (45 C.F.R. 86.41).

3. Participation of Students with Disabilities

A disabled student's right to participate in athletics must be balanced against the school district's responsibility to protect the physical well-being of the student. **Grube v. Bethlehem** deals with this issue.

Grube v. Bethlehem Area Sch. Dist.
550 F. Supp. 418 (E.D. Pa. 1982)

Topic: Participation of Students with Disabilities in Athletic Activities

Facts: Richard Grube is a senior at Freedom High School in the Bethlehem Area School District. He is a vigorous, athletically inclined student who has participated in football since the age of eight. He also engaged in other athletics, such as skiing, tennis, baseball, and wrestling. Richard was qualified by virtue of athletic ability to play in his high school's varsity football team, but he was barred from the football team solely as a result of his lack of one kidney.

Section 504 of the Rehabilitation Act of 1973 ("Act") provides: "No otherwise qualified handicapped individual in the United States . . . shall, solely by reason of his handicap, be excluded from the participation in, be denied the benefits of, or be subjected to discrimination under any program or activity receiving Federal financial assistance."

Issue: Whether the risk of injury is significant enough to make this concern justify the school district's decision in precluding Richard from participating as a member of the high school football team.

Holding: No, Richard is a handicapped individual within the meaning of the Rehabilitation Act of 1973. His selection for the football team established that he is otherwise qualified to play football. *Grube*, 550 F. Supp. at 424. The school district's refusal to permit Richard to participate on the football team lacks substantial justification. There is a strong showing that the school district violated the Act, therefore, a preliminary injunction issued against the school is proper.

Reasoning:

Major Premise: Section 504 of the Rehabilitation Act of 1973 was interpreted by the Supreme Court to mean that an "otherwise qualified" person is "one who is able to meet all of a program's requirements in spite of his handicap." *Grube*, 550 F. Supp. at 422.

Minor Premise: The Act supports the assertion that a handicapped person cannot be denied participation from a sport solely because of his handicap.

Conclusion: Richard is "otherwise qualified" as that language is used in the Act. *Id*. at 425. Thus, he cannot be excluded from participating in the school's football team based solely on his handicap.

IX. DISCIPLINARY ACTION FOR OUT-OF-SCHOOL OFFENSES

With regard to out-of-school conduct, the school district must balance its control of the student's conduct that is necessary for the orderly operation of the school with its obligation to comply with the standards of constitutionality and reasonableness required by the courts to ensure that students receive just and fair treatment.

Although the court agreed that school authorities may discipline students for out-of-school fighting, punishment, such as expulsion, may not be based on unsigned and unidentified statements by student witnesses. See *Tibbs v. Board of Education of the Township of Franklin*, 276 A.2d 165 (N.J. Super, Ct. 1971).

In *Mc Naughton v. Circleville Board of Education*, 345 N.E. 2d 649 (Ohio Comm. Pleas 1974), an Ohio appellate court upheld the suspension from school and from participation in athletic activities of students who held an out-of-school initiation and hazing of new members of an officially recognized high school club. The club's advisor had not been notified nor was he present at the initiation, which occurred at the home of one of the offending students.

Drinking off campus has been addressed by the courts in *Warren v. National Association of Secondary School Principals*, 375 F.Supp. 1043 (Texas 1974), where dismissal from the National Honor Society was upheld.

R.R. v. Board of Education of the Shore Regional High School District, 263 A.2d 180 (N.J. Super. Ct. Ch. Div. 1970), dealt with the issue of whether public school officials can deprive a student of his or her right to attend school because of criminal acts committed off school premises. In this instance, a fifteen-year-old boy stabbed a girl during an altercation in a neighbor's house after the boy had returned home at the end of a school day. This court concluded that officials do have the right to expel or suspend students for out-of-school activities when it is reasonably necessary either for the transgressing student's physical or emotional safety and well-being or for the safety and well-being of other students, teachers, or public school property. Despite this conclusion, the court ordered the school to readmit the student because of due process violations.

In an interesting case where the school district was permitted to discipline a student who was acquitted of reckless driving charges on a technicality, the penalty of the school was upheld because the student had purposely impeded the progress of a school bus, which the courts argued had an effect on the general welfare of the students on the bus and the school in general. See *Clements v. Board of Trustees of the Sheridan County School District No. 2*, 585 P.2d 197 (Wyo. 1978).

With regard to apparent double jeopardy and self-incrimination in these cases where both the criminal courts and the schools are imposing penalties for the same offense, the courts have consistently held that such sanctions by both bodies are not a violation of the student's Fifth Amendment rights. They maintain that school hearing and criminal proceedings have different purposes, with school responses being civil or remedial while judicial responses are punitive. Although acknowledging that school discipline has punitive effects, the courts contend that its underlying purpose is the protection of the school environment. A similar non-school example of this thinking is the prohibiting of Pete Rose's entrance into the Baseball Hall of Fame for gambling even after he served a prison term for the crime.

A meta-analysis of judicial cases reveals that courts have supported the rationale that students may be subject to school discipline, including suspension or expulsion, if their out-of-school conduct threatens the efficient operation of the school. Generally, the courts recognize that the authority to make and enforce policies designed to protect the safety and welfare of student is reasonable and necessary. Of course, these policies should be clearly enunciated in the student handbook. Nevertheless, courts will support the use of that authority only when they perceive the conduct as having a direct and substantial impact on the school and its students.

Chapter Five

Teachers and the Law

Although teachers have not always been successful in actions brought before the courts, their willingness to do so makes them a force to contend with and requires administrators to treat them in a more legally defensible manner.

This chapter deals with the law relating to contract nonrenewal and dismissal of teachers; teachers' freedom of expression; academic freedom; drug testing; standards of dress; the teacher as exemplar; employment discrimination; collective bargaining; and the political rights of teachers.

I. CONTRACT NONRENEWAL AND DISMISSAL

State statutory provisions, teacher union contracts, and case law have provided teachers with safeguards against arbitrary and capricious dismissal. However, according to **Board of Regents of State Colleges v. Roth**, a non-tenured teacher need not be given reasons for non-renewal unless the non-renewal deprived the teacher of a "liberty" interest or if there was a "property" interest in continued employment.

On the other hand, dismissal of a tenured teacher or one under a continuing contract must be made in conformance with the state law. State provisions usually contain grounds for dismissal such as nonperformance of duty, incompetency, insubordination, and conviction of crimes involving moral turpitude. Of course, no action can be taken without proper and appropriate due process.

This relationship between public school teachers and their employers contrasts significantly with that of nonpublic school teachers and their employers. Unless the nonpublic school teacher is covered by a local teacher's contract, none of these due process and equal protection privileges applies.

Board of Regents of State Colleges v. Roth
408 U.S. 564, 92 S. Ct. 2701, 33 L. Ed. 2d 548 (1972)

Topic: Contract Non-renewal and Dismissal

Facts: David Roth, a non-tenured assistant professor at Wisconsin State University-Oshkosh, was hired for a fixed term of one academic year. He completed the academic year, but was informed that he would not be rehired for the next academic year. He was given no reason for the decision not to rehire him, nor was he given any opportunity for a hearing to challenge the decision.

Issue: Whether the failure of University officials to give him notice of any reason for non-retention and an opportunity for a hearing violated his right to procedural due process under the Fourteenth Amendment.

Holding: No, a person is not deprived of his "liberty interest" when he simply is not rehired in one job but remains as free as before to seek another. *See Roth*, 408 U.S. at 575. Similarly, a non-tenured college teacher has no claim of entitlement to re-employment. *See id.* at 578. Therefore, he did not have a "property interest" sufficient to require the University authorities to give him a hearing when they declined to renew his contract of employment. *See id.*

Reasoning:

Major Premise: The requirements of procedural due process apply only to the deprivation of interests encompassed by the Fourteenth Amendment's protection of liberty and property. 408 U.S. at 569.

Minor Premise: Absent any stigma against the non-tenured teacher, or disability foreclosing other employment, the teacher's is not deprived of his "liberty interest." *See id.* at 573. The procedural protection afforded a non-tenured teacher, to protect his "property interest," is limited to the extent of his one-year term of employment. *See id.* at 567.

Conclusion: The non-retention of David Roth is not tantamount to a deprivation of a "liberty interest," and the terms of his employment do not accord him any "property interest" protected by the procedural due process requirement of the Fourteenth Amendment.

II. FREEDOM OF EXPRESSION

The right of educators to freedom of expression has been affected by the belief held in the first half of the 20th century that it was considered a privilege rather than a right to be a public employee. Although this distinction has been modified over the years, the belief that public employment was a privilege had received considerable credibility as a result of Chief Justice Oliver Wendell Holmes' statement, "The petitioner may have a constitutional right to talk politics, but he has no constitutional right to be a policeman. Formal restrictions of government employees' political activities were embodied in the Hatch Act at the federal level and by state statutes at the local level."

Like many other issues that we have seen, the freedom of expression issue as it impacts teachers was revisited during the 1960s. Several teachers challenged the position that they had a limited right of freedom of expression. In **Pickering v. Board of Education of Township High School District 205**, the United States Supreme Court established the principle that public school teachers have the First Amendment right of freedom of expression. Pickering was dismissed from his teaching position for writing a letter, published in a newspaper, critical of several of the school board's actions. These included misallocation of school funds between educational and athletic programs and the board's and the superintendent's methods of informing, or not informing, the school district's taxpayers of the real reasons why additional tax revenues were being sought for the schools. In attempting to balance the teacher's interest as a citizen in making public comments, against the state's interest in promoting the efficiency of its employees' public services, the court struck the balance on the side of the teachers, the so-called Pickering Balance.

In **Mt. Healthy City School District Board of Education v. Doyle**, the Supreme Court decision involving an untenured teacher who had been in an altercation with a colleague, argued with school cafeteria employees, swore at students, and made obscene gestures to female pupils, the Court reasoned that the proper test in such a case is whether or not the school board would have rehired the teacher even in "the absence of the protected conduct." Doyle, the teacher, also called a radio station and provided them with a memorandum from the principal relating to teacher dress and appearance. He alleged that his not being rehired was due to his exercising his First Amendment rights in calling the radio station. The Court obviously disagreed. They believed that he was dismissed because of his unprofessional conduct.

A. Tenured Teacher's Freedom of Expression

Pickering v. Bd. of Educ. of Township High Sch.
391 U.S. 563, 88 S. Ct. 1731, 20 L. Ed. 2d 811 (1968)

Topic: Freedom of Expression

Facts: A teacher wrote a letter to the editor of a local newspaper criticizing the way in which the board of education handled past proposals to raise new revenue for the schools. Specifically, the letter attacked the allocation of financial resources between the school's educational and athletic programs. It also charged the superintendent's attempt to prevent teachers in the district from opposing or criticizing the proposed bond issue. In response, the School Board determined that the letter's publication was detrimental to the efficient operation and administration of the schools in the district. Moreover, the Board decided that the interests of the school required the teacher's dismissal.

Issue: Whether the particular statements made by the teacher are protected by the First Amendment's freedom of expression, and the termination of employment is violative of the teacher's constitutional right to free speech.

Holding: Yes, in the absence of proof of false statements knowingly or recklessly made by him, a teacher's right to speak on issues of public importance could not be the basis for dismissal from public employment. *See Pickering*, 391 U.S. at 574–75.

Reasoning:

Major Premise: The public interest in a free debate on matters of public importance—the core value of the Free Speech Clause of the First Amendment—is so great that it has been held that a State cannot authorize the recovery of damages by a public official for defamatory statements directed at him except when such statements are shown to have been made either with knowledge of their falsity or with reckless disregard for their truth or falsity. *See* 391 U.S. at 573.

Minor Premise: Teachers may not be compelled to relinquish the First Amendment rights they would otherwise enjoy as citizens to comment on matters of public interest in connection with the operation of the public schools in which they work. *See id.* at 568.

Conclusion: Under the free speech clause of the First Amendment, a teacher's exercise of his right to speak on issues of public importance may not furnish the basis for his dismissal from public employment, in the absence of proof of false statements knowingly or recklessly made by him. *See id.* at 574–75.

Notes

The **Pickering** opinion was written by Justice Thurgood Marshall, who argued the famous desegregation case, **Brown v. Board of Education of Topeka**. He was the first African American to be named to the Supreme Court. He had been counsel for the National Association for the Advancement of Colored People and the NSSCP Legal Defense and Educational Fund for twenty-five years, having won twenty-nine out of thirty-two cases that he argued before the Supreme Court. He was replaced in 1991 by Clarence Thomas.

Subsequent decisions to **Pickering** have discussed a two-step process to determine whether a teacher's speech has First Amendment protection. First, the disputed speech must address a matter of public concern. Second, the interests of the teacher must be balanced against the interests of the state as employer in rendering a public service through its employees. The second determination, known as the Pickering Balance, may be based on: (1) the need for harmony in the office or work place; (2) the need for a close working relationship between the speaker and co-workers and whether the speech in question undermines that relationship; (3) the time, place, and manner of the speech; (4) the context in which a dispute arises; (5) the degree of public interest in the speech; and (6) whether the speech impedes the employee's ability to perform his or her duties. See *Roberts v. Van Buren Public Schools,* 773 F.2d 949 (8th Cir. 1985), *Cox v. Dardanelle Public School District,* 790 F.2d 668 (8th Cir. 1986), and *Day v. South Park Independent School District,* 768 F.2d 696 (5th Cir. 1985).

Pickering does not apply to nonpublic schools because they are not government institutions. The rights of nonpublic school teachers would be determined by the individual contracts and labor agreements that they may have. A nonpublic school was upheld, for example, in its dismissal of a high school teacher who wore a beard in violation of the school's rules. The school's participation in a state-operated teacher pension fund did not sufficiently bring the school under government auspices. See *Johnson v. Pinkerton Academy,* 861 F.2d 335 (1st Cir. 1988).

B. Nontenured Teacher's Freedom of Expression

Mt. Healthy City Bd. Of Educ. v. Doyle
429 U.S. 274, 97 S. Ct. 568, 50 L. Ed. 2d 471 (1977)

Topic: Nontenured Teacher's Freedom of Expression

Facts: An untenured teacher communicated the substance of the school principal's memorandum on teacher dress and appearance to a local radio station. This memorandum was apparently prompted by the view of some in the administration that there was a relationship between teacher appearance and public support for bond issues. The radio station used the communication in a newscast.

Previously, the teacher had been involved in an altercation with another teacher, an argument with school cafeteria employees, an incident in which he swore at students, and in an incident in which he made obscene gestures to female students. Thereafter, the school board advised the teacher that he would not be rehired and cited his lack of tact in handling professional matters, with specific mention of the radio station and obscene gesture incidents.

Issue: Whether the refusal to rehire the teacher violated his rights under the First Amendment.

Holding: A teacher may establish a claim for reinstatement if the decision not to rehire him was made by reason of his exercise of constitutionally protected First Amendment freedoms. *Doyle,* 429 U.S. at 283–84. However, the board's decision not to rehire the teacher does not amount to a constitutional violation if the board would have reached the same decision (i.e., not to renew the teacher's contract) had the constitutionally protected incident (i.e., communication to the radio station) not occurred. *Id.* at 285.

Reasoning:

Major Premise: A teacher's claim under the First Amendment is not defeated by the fact that he did not have tenure.

Minor Premise: Because a teacher engaged in a constitutionally protected conduct, it will not prevent the school board from discharging him on the basis his performance record. *Id.* at 285–286.

Conclusion: A teacher ought not to be able, by engaging in constitutionally protected conduct, to prevent his employer from assessing his performance record and reaching a decision not to rehire on the basis of that record, simply because the protected conduct makes the employer more certain of the correctness of its decision. *Id.* at 286.

Notes

Doyle reaffirmed the understanding that non-tenured teachers do have First Amendment rights of freedom of expression, and they may establish a claim to reinstatement if these rights have been violated. However, engaging in constitutionally protected conduct may not prevent an employer from discharging a teacher on the basis of his or her total performance. Prior to this decision, some very savvy teachers were alleged to purposely engage in protected activities in order to claim that such action was the reason for their dismissal and not their poor performance.

III. ACADEMIC FREEDOM

Litigation often occurs when a school district's views regarding academic freedom are incongruent with a teacher's perception of autonomy in determining the materials, methods, and topics in a particular class. In this type of litigation, teachers generally allege that they have a constitutional right to present material to which students, parents, or school officials may object. Although courts have recognized that teachers have such academic freedom, it is not absolute.

A. Appropriate Materials

Fowler v. Bd. Of Educ. Of Lincoln County
819 F.2d 657 (6th Cir. 1987)

Topic: Academic Freedom—Appropriate Materials

Facts: Jacqueline Fowler, a tenured teacher, was fired by the Board of Education for insubordination and conduct unbecoming a teacher. The basis for this termination was that the teacher had an "R" rated movie, *Pink-Floyd—-The Wall*, shown to her high school students on the last day of the 1983–1984 school year. Students in Fowler's class were between the ages of fourteen and seventeen. The movie contained offensive language, violence, and nudity.

The film was shown on a non-instructional day as "treat" for students. Fowler had not previously seen the film, left the room on several occasions while film was being shown, and made no attempt to explain any message students might derive from viewing it.

Issue: Whether the termination of Fowler's employment was in violation of the First Amendment right to freedom of speech and expression.

Holding: No, Fowler's conduct in having the movie shown was not expressive or communicative and did not constitute expression protected by the First Amendment.

Reasoning:

Major Premise: Conduct is protected by the First Amendment only when it is expressive or communicative in nature. *Fowler*, 819 F.2d at 664.

Minor Premise: The showing of a sexually explicit movie without proper instruction was neither educationally communicative nor expressive. *Id*.

Conclusion: The showing of a sexually explicit movie without proper instruction is not protected by the First Amendment. *Id*.

Notes

For academic freedom defenses to succeed, it must be shown that the teacher did not defy legitimate state and local curriculum directives, followed accepted professional norms for that grade level and subject matter, discussed matters that were of public concern, and acted professionally and in good faith when there was no precedent or policy. Thus, although teachers' academic freedom is protected, it has definite limits.

There is evidence that academic freedom may be bargained away in a teacher's collective bargaining contract. A contract that had a provision that the board shall have the right to "determine the processes, techniques, methods, and means of teaching any and all subjects" was challenged by English teachers when the board tried to censor certain books. The court held for the school board but contended it would have held for the teachers if the negotiated agreement had not existed. See *Cary v. Board of Education of Adams—Arapahoe School District 28-J*, 598 F.2d 535 (10th Cir. 1979).

B. Political Speakers

Wilson v. Chancellor
418 F. Supp. 1358 (D. Or. 1976)

Topic: Political Speakers

Facts: A teacher, as part of his political science class at Molalla Union High School, invited a Communist to speak to his class. The teacher, Dean Wilson, already and without objection had presented a Democrat, a Republican, and a member of the John Birch Society. Before the Communist could speak to the class, the Board issued an order banning "all political speakers" from the high school.

Issue: Whether the order "all political speakers" violates the First Amendment and the equal protection clause of the Fourteenth Amendment.

Holding: Yes, a public high school teacher's use of political speakers in his class was his medium for teaching, and the ban on "all political speakers" from school interfered with that medium, thus the ban operated to suppress the teacher's freedom of expression under the First Amendment. *Wilson*, 418 F. Supp. at 1363–64.

Reasoning:

Major Premise: A teacher's teaching is an expression to which the First Amendment applies. *Id*. at 1362.

Minor Premise: The act of teaching is a form of expression, and the methods used in teaching are media. *Id*. at 1363.

Conclusion: The ban on "all political speakers" interfered with the teacher's medium for teaching, and it operated to suppress the teacher's freedom of expression under the First Amendment. *Id*. at 1363–64.

IV. DRUG TESTING

With the prevalence of drugs in American society, some school districts have adopted drug screening policies for teachers. Based on a 1966 Supreme Court decision, however, courts construe mandatory urine sampling as a search and, thus, subject to the Fourth Amendment's protection against unreasonable searches. Thus, in order to test for drugs, there needs to be reasonable cause. See *Schmerber v. California*, 384 U.S. 757 (1966).

In determining the reasonableness of a drug search, the courts consider several factors: (1) the intrusiveness of the search, (2) the necessity of conducting the search, and (3) the degree of suspicion that triggered the search. The need to screen teachers, for example, has been found to be less compelling that the need to test school bus drivers for drugs. Thus, the courts have routinely banned the blanket drug testing of teachers. However, only reasonable cause needs to shown, not the more demanding probable cause.

V. DRESS

Personal appearance of teachers in respect to dress and grooming has received considerable attention in the courts. School authorities generally contend that proper dress and grooming establish a professional image for teachers, promote good grooming among students, and aid in the maintenance of respect and decorum in the classroom. Teachers, on the other hand, generally allege that local regulations governing their personal appearance invade their right of privacy and liberty.

East Hartford Educ. Assoc. v. Bd. Of Educ. Of East Hartford
562 F.2d 838 (2d Cir. 1977)

Topic: Teacher's Rights and School Board Regulations

Facts: A teacher objects to the Board of Education's dress code requiring him to wear a shirt and tie with his sport jacket; he seeks to wear a turtleneck sweater or open-necked sport shirt with his jacket. There is no claim that the teacher's desired dress would cause any disruption of the classroom, any problem of pupil discipline, any challenge to school board curricular authority, or any interference with school operations.

Issue: Whether the dress code violates the First Amendment and the Fourteenth Amendment.

Holding: No, a School Board may impose reasonable regulations governing the appearance of the teachers it employs, and in view of the uniquely influential role of the public teacher in the classroom, the board is justified in imposing this regulation. *East Hartford*, 562 F.2d at 863.

Reasoning:

Major Premise: As conduct becomes less and less like "pure speech," a right protected by the Constitution, the showing of governmental interest required for its regulation is progressively lessened. *Id.* at 858.

Minor Premise: A dress code requiring teachers to dress in a professional manner is a rational means of promoting respect for authority and traditional values, as well as discipline in the classroom. *Id.* at 859.

Conclusion: The School Board's dress code requirement that teacher wear a necktie did not impermissibly infringe upon the teacher's liberty and privacy interests. *Id.* at 861–62.

VI. TEACHER AS ROLE MODEL OR EXEMPLAR

To say that times have changed regarding the expectations of teachers as role models or exemplars is a gross understatement. Take, for example, the Rules of Conduct for Teachers, which was published by a local West Virginia Board of Education in 1915.

Rules of Conduct for Teachers

1. You will not marry during the term of your contract.
2. You are not to keep company with men.
3. You must be home between the hours of 8:00 pm and 6:00 am unless attending a school function.
4. You may not loiter downtown in ice cream stores.
5. You may not travel beyond the city limits unless you have the permission of the chairman of the board.

6. You may not ride in a carriage or automobile with any man unless he is your father or brother.
7. You may not smoke cigarettes.
8. You may not dress in bright colors.
9. You may under no circumstances dye your hair.
10. You must wear at least two petticoats.
11. Your dresses must not be any shorter than two inches above the ankle.
12. To keep the schoolroom neat and clean, you must sweep the floor at least once daily; scrub the floor at least once a week with hot, soapy water; clean the blackboards at least once a day, and start the fire at 7:00 am so the room will be warm by 8:00 am.

Obviously, these rules have become obsolete over the years, but they indicate the continuing belief that teachers should act as role models for their students and the community.

In the contemporary world, changing standards and norms regarding proper behavior make it difficult for educators to know with any kind of certainty what the community's expectations of them as exemplars are. These standards vary from community to community. If one is teaching in the "Bible Belt," for example, the expected standards of behavior vary significantly with those of the Northeast or West Coast.

It is not at all uncommon for state statutes and school system policies to cite immorality or moral turpitude as grounds for disciplinary action, or even dismissal. Therefore, courts have been required to adjudicate cases dealing with controversial lifestyles. Some of these issues have included homosexuality, adultery, unmarried members of the opposite sex living together, unwed pregnant teachers, sex-change operations, and sexual advances by teachers toward students. The overriding factor in the adjudication of these cases is whether the questionable conduct negatively affects the teacher's performance or the student's learning.

Up to now the courts have been somewhat inconsistent in their treatment of some of these issues, but we have selected some cases that reflect the general court opinion on these topics.

A. Homosexual Teacher

In the earliest cases dealing with claims by homosexual teachers of their denial of a teaching position, dismissal, or certificate revocation, court decisions generally upheld the school authorities. However, several recent decisions have tended to uphold the rights of homosexual teachers. And, in several states and localities laws have been passed to protect homosexuals' employment rights. **Gaylord** is an example of an earlier case.

Gaylord v. Tacoma Sch. Dist. No. 10
559 P.2d 1340 (Wash. 1977) (en banc), *cert. denied*, 434 U.S. 879 (1977)

Topic: Discharge of Homosexual Teacher

Facts: A school district policy provides for discharge of school employees for "immorality." Under the school board's policy, the board may discharge teachers for "sufficient cause."

Gaylord was a teacher at Wilson High School. A former student told the school's vice-principal that he thought Gaylord was a homosexual. The vice-principal confronted Gaylord at his home with a written copy of the student's statement. Mr. Gaylord admitted he was a homosexual and attempted unsuccessfully to have the vice-principal drop the matter. Subsequently, the Tacoma School Board found that there was probable cause for Gaylord's discharge based on his status as a publicly known homosexual.

Issue: Whether substantial evidence supports the findings that, as a known homosexual, Gaylord's fitness as a teacher was impaired to the injury of the Wilson High School, and therefore his discharge was justified.

Holding: Yes, substantial evidence supported the conclusion that Gaylord was guilty of immorality and that, as a known homosexual, his fitness as a teacher was impaired to the injury of the high school in which he taught, justifying his discharge. *Gaylord*, 559 P.2d at 1347.

Reasoning:

Major Premise: Homosexuality is "immoral" within the school board policy providing for discharge of employees for "immorality." 559 P.2d at 1343–44.

Minor Premise: If a homosexual teacher is not discharged after he became known as a homosexual, it would impair his teaching efficiency. *Id.* at 1342.

Conclusion: Gaylord was properly discharged based upon his admission and disclosure that he was a homosexual.

Notes

The issue of gay rights continues to be topical in today's society. Several anti-gay-rights laws have been challenged in the courts. A ruling by the Hawaii supreme court contended that Hawaii's ban on same-sex marriage "is presumed to be unconstitutional" unless the state can show that the prohibition is "justified by compelling state interests." See *Baehr v. Lewin*, 852 F.2d 44 (Haw. 1993). The military has adopted a "don't ask, don't tell" policy for homosexuals. Kentucky has struck down its sodomy criminal statutes, *Kentucky v. Wasson*, 842 S.W.2d 487 (Ky. 1992). Several states and the District of Columbia have passed laws prohibiting discrimination on the basis of sexual orientation in such areas as employment, housing, public accommodations, education, and credit.

Homosexual teachers have prevailed in two decisions decided in the late 1990s. In *Glover v. Williamburg Local School District Board of Education*, a gay teacher claimed his non-renewal was based on discrimination because of his sexual orientation. The court found that administrators and board members had acted on the basis of false rumors that he had held hands at school with his partner during a holiday party. In its decision, the court criticized the defendants for accepting the rumor as fact, not confronting Glover with the rumors, lowering evaluations of Glover due in large part to the defendants' reliance on false rumors, and board members' testimony that was contradictory and not entirely credible. The court held that he was discriminated against by the board's action and stated that: "Homosexuals, while not a 'suspect class' for equal protection analysis, are entitled to at least the same protection as any other identifiable group which is subject to disparate treatment by the state." In *Weaver v. Nebo School District*, a school district sought to restrict a lesbian teacher's right to express her sexual orientation outside the classroom in addition to not rehiring her as volleyball coach. In its decision, the court found that the community's perception about Weaver, based on nothing more than unsupported assumptions, outdated stereotypes, and animosity did not furnish a rational basis for not rehiring her as volleyball coach. Regarding her free speech restriction, the court held: "As impermissible as it is to restrict a state employee's right to speak on a matter of public concern, it is equally impermissible to retaliate against that employee when he or she does indeed speak on a matter of public concern." The court ordered that Weaver be offered the volleyball coaching position and that letters requesting her not to discuss her homosexuality be removed from her personnel file.

Striking down sodomy statutes, allowing same-sex marriages, and passing laws that prohibit discrimination based on sexual orientation, have significant import for public school educators. It will be virtually impossible to have measures restricting the hiring of homosexuals or the dismissal of practicing homosexuals stand up to a court challenge.

B. Adulterous Behavior

Erb v. Iowa State Bd. Of Pub. Instruction

216 N.W.2d 339 (Iowa 1974), *superseded by statute on other grounds*, 256 N.W.2d 913 (Iowa 1977)

Topic: Adulterous Teacher

Facts: Erb, a native Iowan, military veteran, and holder of a master's degree in fine arts, received his Iowa teaching certificate in 1963. A complaint against Erb was made by Robert M. Johnson, a farmer whose wife Margaret taught home economics in the Nishna Valley school. At a hearing of the Board of Educational Examiners ("Board"), Johnson read an extensive statement in which he detailed his observations relating to an adulterous liaison between Erb and Johnson's wife, which began and ended in spring 1970.

Erb offered to resign his teaching position, but the local school board unanimously decided not to accept his resignation. The local school board president testified that Erb's teaching was highly rated by his principal and superintendent, he had been forgiven by his wife and the student body, and he had maintained the respect of the community. Witnesses before the Board included Erb's past and present high school principals, his minister, a parent of children in the school, and a substitute teacher. All vouched for his character and fitness to teach. However, the Board voted five to four to revoke Erb's teaching certificate.

Issue: Whether there is substantial evidence in the record that would have supported revocation if the proper standard had been applied?

Holding: No, the teacher's adultery was not ground for the revocation of the teaching certificate in absence of evidence that the isolated occurrence in an otherwise unblemished past would have an adverse effect on fitness to teach. *Erb*, 216 N.W.2d at 344.

Reasoning:

Major Premise: The sole purpose of the Board of Educational Examiners to revoke teaching certificates is to provide a means of protecting the school community from harm, and its exercise is unlawful for any other purpose. *Id.*

Minor Premise: A teaching certificate can only be revoked upon a showing before the Board of a reasonable likelihood that the teacher's retention in the profession will adversely affect the school community. *Id.*

Conclusion: A teacher's admitted adultery would not support a revocation of teaching certificate in the absence of evidence that the isolated occurrence in an otherwise unblemished past would adversely affect the school community. *Id.*

C. Criminal Activities

McBroom v. Bd. of Educ., Dist. No. 205
494 N.E. 2d 1191 (Ill. App. Ct. 1986)

Topic: Criminal Activities

Facts: Nance McBroom was a tenured physical education teacher employed by the school district for approximately 12 years. She was the chairperson of the girl's physical education department at York High School during the 1982–83 school term.

On May 9, 1983, while checking and straightening the girl's locker room, McBroom found an endorsed check for $290 in a wastebasket. The check was payable to a student, Marci Spaulding, and her mother Beverly Spaulding. McBroom knew Kelly Spaulding, Marci's sister. McBroom made no effort to return the check, instead, she took the check to her bank. At the bank, McBroom requested the teller to cash the $290 check. However, Marci had notified the bank that the check had been stolen. Consequently, the bank refused payment and retained possession of the check.

Later that day, McBroom was arrested at the high school by an Elmhurst police officer for theft of the check. On November 8, 1983, McBroom pled guilty to theft of the check and was sentenced to pay a fine and placed under court supervision. This incident was widely reported in the *Elmhurst Press*, the only local newspaper in Elmhurst. Elmhurst is a city of approximately 44,000 residents. Subsequently, McBroom was dismissed by the school district, without written warning, for theft of the $290 social security check. McBroom appealed her dismissal.

Issue: Whether there is just cause to justify the dismissal of the tenured teacher.

Holding: Yes, McBroom's criminal conduct and other aggravating factors constitute sufficient cause to warrant discharge. *McBroom*, 494 N.E.2d at 1196. In addition, the tenured teacher's criminal conduct was irremediable, as the concept of remediable conduct was not intended to apply to criminal conduct that has no legitimate basis in our society. *Id.* at 1198.

Reasoning:

Major Premise: A tenured teacher can be dismissed upon showing of just cause. *See* 494 N.E.2d at 1195. Where no warning is given for a tenured teacher's dismissal, the Board of Education must provide evidence that the teacher's conduct is irremediable. *Id.* at 1198.

Minor Premise: There is substantial evidence to support a finding of cause for dismissal: (1) "the special position of leadership occupied by a teacher who serves as a role model and instills the basic values of our society"; (2) McBroom's students are at an impressionable age; (3) McBroom's "credibility and effectiveness in teaching students honesty and ethical values was substantially impaired as a result of her misconduct and notoriety in the community."; (4) McBroom's leadership position, as chairperson of the girl's physical education department, magnified future difficulty; and (5) theft is a significant problem at the high school. *Id.* at 1196. The concept of remediable conduct was not intended to apply to criminal conduct. *Id.* at 1198. "Teachers, as leaders and role models, with their education and background, have the duty to implant basic societal values and qualities of good citizenship in their students." *Id.*

Conclusion: There is just cause for dismissal and the criminal conduct is irremediable.

D. Impropriety with Students

Barcheski v. Bd. of Educ. of Grand Rapids Pub. Sch.
412 N.W.2d 296 (Mich. Ct. App. 1987)

Topic: Impropriety with Students

Facts: Robert Barcheski was a tenured teacher in the Grand Rapids Public Schools at the close of the 1971–72 school year. On or about August 10, 1976, Mr. Barcheski invited two female students of his driver education class to a party to be held on Friday, August 13, 1976, the night before the raft race. At the party, the two female students, Mary and Wendy, drank beer and smoked pot in the presence of Mr. Barcheski.

After the party, Mr. Barcheski took Mary home. Mary was 15 years of age at that time. Consequently, Mr. Barcheski was discharged.

Issue: Whether the proof received by the school board, or the tenure commission, or both, supports the findings that Mr. Barcheski was discharged based on reasonable and just cause.

Holding: Yes, the finding that (1) Mr. Barcheski invited at least one female student to the party; and (2) that the two female students drank beer and smoked marijuana in Mr. Barcheski's presence at the party, was supported by competent, material, and substantial evidence. *Barcheski*, 412 N.W.2d at 300-301. Moreover, Mr. Barcheski "was, or should have been, well aware that taking Mary, a young, intoxicated female student home alone in his car constituted, by itself, grounds for discipline." *Id*. at 302.

Reasoning:

Major Premise: A tenured teacher may be discharged based on reasonable and just cause, such as improprieties with students.

Minor Premise: Mr. Barcheski was "adequately put on notice that driving Mary home alone constituted by itself conduct supporting a charge of improper or wrongful conduct." 412 N.W.2d at 303.

Conclusion: Mr. Barcheski was discharged based on reasonable and just cause.

Gebser v. Loga Vista Indep. Sch. Dist.
118 S. Ct. 1989 (1998)

Topic: Liability for Impropriety with Students

Facts: Alida Star Gebser, an eighth-grade student at a middle school in Logo Vista Independent School District, had a sexual relationship with her teacher, Frank Waldrop. Gebser did not report the relationship to school officials. After a police officer discovered Waldrop and Gebser engaging in sexual intercourse and the teacher was arrested, Logo Vista terminated Waldrop's employment. Gebser and her mother filed suit against Logo Vista claiming for damages under Title IX of the Education Amendments of 1972. Title IX provides in pertinent part that, "[n]o person . . . shall, on the basis of sex, be excluded from participation in, be denied benefits of, or be subjected to discrimination under any education program or activity receiving Federal financial assistance." 118 S. Ct. at 1994 (citing 20 U.S.C. § 1681(a)).

Issue: Whether a school district may be held liable in damages, without actual notice, in an implied right of action under Title IX of the Education Amendments of 1972 for the sexual harassment of a student by one of the district's teachers.

Holding: No, damages may not be recovered for teacher–student sexual harassment in an implied private right of action under Title IX "unless an official of the school district who at a minimum has authority to institute corrective measures on the district's behalf has actual notice of, and is deliberately indifferent to, the teacher's misconduct." *Gebser*, 118 S. Ct. at 1993.

Reasoning:

Major Premise: The express means of enforcement under Title IX—by administrative agencies—operates on an assumption of actual notice to officials of the funding recipient. *Id*. at 1998. Moreover, the "administrative enforcement scheme presupposes that an official who is advised of a Title IX violation refuses to take action to bring the recipient into compliance." *Id*. at 1999.

Minor Premise: It would "frustrate the purposes of Title IX to permit damages recovery against a school district for a teacher's sexual harassment of a student based on principles of constructive notice, i.e., without actual notice to a school district official." *Id*. at 1997 (internal quotation marks omitted).

Conclusion: Damage claims under Title IX require that a school district official must have actual knowledge about a teacher's sexual harassment and failed to adequately respond. 118 S. Ct. at 1999. Moreover, the official's response must amount to deliberate indifference to discrimination. *Id.*

Notes

In *Knowles v. Board of Education,* 857 P.2d 553 (Colo.Ct. App. 1993), the dismissal of a tenured middle school teacher accused of "inappropriate conduct" was upheld. The teacher had made repeated offensive sexual statements toward female students and placed his hand on a student's back and snapped her bra strap.

In *Moore v. Knowles,* 482 F.d 1069 (5th Cur. 1973), a teacher's dismissal based on a grand jury's indictment for sexual misconduct with teenage pupils was upheld. Although the teacher was not provided a hearing before the school board to refute the allegations of misconduct, the court ruled that the dismissal did not violate his right of due process. In the event that the school board brought the charges, the court held that the teacher would have been entitled to a hearing before the board.

VII. EMPLOYMENT DISCRIMINATION

Personnel practices that have an impact on racial minorities, women, pregnant women, religious groups, older persons, and people with disabilities have sometimes been challenged as being discriminatory. In addition to constitutional protections under the Fourteenth Amendment's Equal Protection and Due Process Clauses, several federal statutes protect public school personnel against employment discrimination. These statutes include: Sections 1981 through 1983 of Title 42, United States Code; Title IX of the Education amendments of 1972; the Americans with Disabilities Act of 1990 and section 504 of the Rehabilitation Act of 1973; the Pregnancy Discrimination Act of 1978; the Age Discrimination in Employment Act of 1976 and its amendments; and Title VII of the Civil Rights Act of 1964. The Civil Rights Act of 1964, the seminal legislative enactment of the movement to eradicate discrimination in the workplace, provides in part:

SECTION 703
(a) It shall be an unlawful employment practice for an employer
  (1) to discriminate against any individual with respect to his compensation, terms, conditions, or privileges of employment, because of such individual's race, color, religion, sex, or national origin . . .
(b) It shall not be an unlawful employment practice to hire and employ
  Employees on the basis of religion, sex, or national origin in those certain instances where religion, sex, or national origin is a bona fide occupational qualification reasonably necessary to the normal operation of that particular business or enterprise.

A. Racial Discrimination

Racial discrimination against teachers has been a much litigated issue since the Supreme Court's decision in **Brown v. Board of Education of Topeka,** 347 U.S. 483 (1954), in which *de jure* segregation was declared to be a violation of the Equal Protection Clause of the Fourteenth Amendment. Court-ordered desegregation plans subsequent to **Brown** often contain provisions effectively regulating the hiring, promotion, and dismissal of minority school personnel. Courts also may impose affirmative action plans on school districts that have violated Title VII.

Although not a decision dealing with educators, a Supreme Court decision upheld the "last-hired—first-fired" principle as applied to Memphis firefighters. The Court asserted that seniority systems, as long as they are unbiased, may not be disrupted to save the jobs of newly hired minority workers. The decision states: "It is inappropriate to deny an innocent employee the benefits of his seniority in order to provide a remedy in a pattern or practice suit such as this." See *Firefighters Local Union No. 1784 v. Stotts*, 467 U.S. 561 (1984).

The Supreme Court did not uphold a layoff plan that was part of a school district's collective bargaining agreement. Although the plan called for retaining teachers by seniority, it also stipulated that minorities were not to be dismissed in proportions greater than their representation in the district. When, in accordance with the racially sensitive stipulation, Caucasian teachers were terminated instead of less-senior African American teachers, the displaced Caucasian teachers claimed reverse discrimination. The Court agreed, holding that the policy was a violation of the non-minority teachers' constitutional equal protection. Racial classifications such as that imposed by the policy were justified only when narrowly tailored to accomplish a compelling state purpose. However, the Court found that other, less intrusive, means were available to the district to accomplish its purpose—for example, the adoption of hiring goals. Although the policy would have been allowable to remedy past *de jure* discrimination, no such finding had been made in court. See *Wygant v. Jackson Board of Education*, 476 U.S. 267 (1986).

In *United States v. Board of Education of Township of Piscataway*, 832 F.Supp. 836 (N.J. 1993), a federal court rejected an affirmative action plan preferring minority teachers over non-minority teachers when candidates to be laid off appeared to be equally qualified. Under this plan, a Caucasian female business education teacher was laid off, instead of an African American female teacher with the same seniority, solely on the basis of race. The court further contended that Title VII did not require a plan such as this and that it was based merely on a desire to achieve faculty diversity.

In *Jacobson v. Cincinnati Board of Education*, 961 F.2d 100 (6th Cir.1992), a teacher's union challenge to a teacher transfer policy designed to ensure that faculty reflected a system-wide racial balance also was not upheld. In its decision, a federal appellate court contended that although the policy was "race conscious," it was "specific race neutral" and had no disparate impact. The court agreed that in "some instances, it will benefit or harm white teachers; in others, it will benefit or harm black teachers."

The Civil Rights Act of 1991 nullified or modified many Supreme Court decisions where the burden regarding discrimination was placed on the plaintiffs to prove that a policy was the "cause" of the discrimination and not merely the "effect." Under this law, victims of employment bias based on race, sex, disability, religion, or national origin may collect limited compensatory and punitive damages. Damages had heretofore only been available to victims of discrimination based on race. Employment practices under the Civil Rights Act of 1991, must be "job-related for the position in question and consistent with business necessity." Another major purpose of the law was to return to the standard that required employers to prove that an employment standard that results in adverse impact is necessary for successful job performance.

Teacher competency tests have been challenged on the grounds that they can be racially biased. Courts have found that such testing fulfills a legitimate state function, and they have upheld tests and cutoff scores that objective validation has shown to be indicative of actual job qualifications. The decision in *United States v. South Carolina*, 445 F.Supp. 1094 (S.C. 1977), upheld the use of the National Teacher Examination as a requirement for state certification, despite the fact that its use disproportionately disqualified African Americans.

B. Sex Discrimination

Marshall v. Kirkland
602 F.2d 1282 (8th Cir. 1979)

Topic: Sex Discrimination

Facts: Women have predominated as teachers in Barton-Lexa School District. The ratio of women to men was between three and four to one. Evidence was presented indicating that assignment to "specialty" positions and promotion to one of the three administrative positions in the district was influenced by the sex of the employee. These two types of positions statistically favored males, with the concomitant differential in pay between men and women.

"Specialty" positions are positions with extra duties for which a higher compensation was provided. Administrative positions include principal of the elementary school, principal of the high school, and superintendent of the district.

Issue: Whether the evidence presented established a prima facie case of sex discrimination.

Holding: Yes, the evidence was sufficient to show that the school district had a "discernible policy or practice of hiring only men (or women) for certain specific administrative or specialty jobs." *Marshall*, 602 F.2d at 1301.

Reasoning:

Major Premise: A prima facie case of sex discrimination is established where sufficient objective and subjective evidence of discriminatory pattern is presented, accompanied by invidious discriminatory purpose in the assignment and promotion of female teachers. 602 F.2d at 1299.

Minor Premise: At a minimum, a prima facie case is established where it is shown that "decision-makers in the school district sought to maintain women teachers in a 'stereotypic and predefined place' in the school district." *Id.* at 1301.

Conclusion: A prima facie case of sex discrimination is established because the school district had a policy or practice of hiring only men, or women, for certain positions.

Notes

In *Grove City College v. Bell*, 465 U.S. 555 (1984), the Supreme Court, referring to private institutions, declared that Title IX did not apply to schools and colleges as a whole but only to those parts of an institution that received federal aid directly. However, provisions of the Civil Rights Restoration Act of 1988 were designed to overturn the *Grove City College* decision. The act made it clear that if one part of an entity receives federal funds, then the entire entity is covered.

C. Pregnancy

A challenge to local school board policies that provided for mandatory leave at a particular time in a pregnancy and rules pertaining to reemployment after delivery has been heard by the United States Supreme Court. In its decision in *Cleveland Board of Education v. La Fleur*, 414 U.S. 632 (1974), the Court held that mandatory maternity termination provisions stating the number of months before anticipated childbirth violated the Due Process Clause of the Fourteenth Amendment. Additionally, the Court struck down the provision that a mother could not return to work until the next regular semester after her child was three months old.

In the area of fringe benefits, such as disability benefits, sick leave, and health insurance, the same principle applies. A woman unable to work for pregnancy-related reasons is entitled to disability benefits or sick leave on the same basis as employees unable to work for other temporary medical reasons.

Eckmann v. Bd. of Educ. of Hawthorne Sch. Dist. No. 17
636 F. Supp. 1214 (N.D. Ill. 1986)

Topic: Gender Discrimination—Pregnancy

Facts: An Illinois teacher was discharged from her position. The teacher sought compensatory and punitive damages for her allegedly unconstitutional discharge. She claimed that the constitutionally protected conduct that motivated the School Board to dismiss her was her out-of-wedlock pregnancy coupled with her decision to raise her child as a single parent. 636 F. Supp. at 1217.

There are three burdens in this case: (1) the teacher must show some constitutionally protected conduct; (2) the teacher must show that the protected conduct was a "substantial" or "motivating" factor behind the school board's conduct; and (3) the school board must then show by a preponderance of the evidence that it would have taken the same action even if the teacher had not engaged in the constitutionally protected conduct. *Id.*

Issue: Whether the School Board met its burden of proof by showing that it would have dismissed the teacher regardless of the teacher's out-of-wedlock pregnancy and her decision to raise her child as a single parent.

Holding: The evidence supported the findings that the school board's motivation for discharging the teacher was her out-of-wedlock pregnancy and her decision to raise her son as a single mother. *Id.* at 1219–220.

Reasoning:

Major Premise: The individual's decision regarding marriage and child bearing is constitutionally protected from state infringement. *Eckmann*, 636 F. Supp. at 1218.

Minor Premise: Teacher had a substantive due process right to conceive and raise her child out of wedlock without unwarranted intrusion by the school board. *Id.*

Conclusion: Because the evidence supports the finding that the school board's decision to dismiss the teacher was motivated by her out-of-wedlock pregnancy and her decision to raise her child as a single mother, the school board engaged in unconstitutional conduct. *Id.* at 1219–220.

D. Religious Discrimination

The Civil Rights Act of 1964 contains wording that indicates than an employer must "reasonably accommodate to an employee's . . . religious observances or practice without undue hardship on the conduct of the employer's business." In *Ansonia Board of Education v. Philbrook*, 479 U.S.60 (1986), the Court considered a teacher's request to use, for religious purposes, his allotment of "necessary personal business" leave. The teachers' bargaining agreement allowed three days of paid religious leave not included among the enumerated reasons for taking leave for personal business. The school board required the teacher to take unpaid leave for all religious observances exceeding three days. Upholding the board, the Court declared the policy to be a "reasonable accommodation" under Title VII of the Civil Rights Act.

A Pennsylvania law prohibiting the wearing of religious garb while teaching in a public school was challenged in *United States v. Board of Education for the School District of Philadelphia*, 911 F.2d 882 (3rd Cir. 1990). A Muslim teacher who had the conviction that Muslim women should cover their entire body, except for their hands and face, while in public, challenged the law under Title VII. A federal appellate court upheld the school district's refusal to allow her to wear such dress. The court ruled that the preservation of an atmosphere of religious neutrality in the public schools is a compelling state interest justifying statutes prohibiting teachers from wearing religious garb while teaching.

A federal appellate court struck down a requirement that teachers in a Protestant school be Protestant. In *EEOC v. Kamelhameha Schools/Bishop Estate*, 990 F.2d 458 (9th Cir. 1993), cert. denied, 510 U.S. 963 (1993), the court reasoned that except for the school's theology courses, other teachers at the school had provided instruction in a secular way and there was nothing that they taught that would require them to be of the Protestant faith. This is an interesting decision in light of the aid to nonpublic school cases where contributing to the salaries of teachers who taught secular subjects was unconstitutional because it violated the separation of church and state. See *Lemon v. Kurtzman,* 403 U.S. 602 (1971).

E. Age Discrimination

The Age Discrimination in Employment Act of 1967 prohibits an employer from discriminating against an employee or potential employee on the basis of age, except "where age is a bona fide occupational qualification reasonably necessary to the normal operation of the particular business, or where the differentiation is based on reasonable factors other than age." Coverage of the act is limited to employees within the ages of forty and seventy, and there is no upper limit for federal workers and teachers in higher education.

One of the typical cases regarding age discrimination as it applies to teachers is **Geller v. Markham.**

Geller v. Markham
635 F.2d 1027 (2d Cir. 1980)

Topic: Age Discrimination

Facts: Miriam Geller, a 55-year-old teacher, applied for a job at Bugbee School in West Hartford in August 1976. She had considerable experience as a tenured teacher in New Jersey. She was told to begin teaching art on September 7. However, school officials continued to interview other candidates for the job. On September 17, Ms. Geller was replaced by a 25-year-old woman who had not applied for a job until September 10.

West Hartford had a cost-cutting "Sixth Step Policy." This policy read: "Except in special situations and to the extent possible, teachers needed in West Hartford next year will be recruited at levels below the sixth step of the salary schedule." 635 F.2d at 1030. the "sixth step" salary grade consists of teachers with more than five years' experience.

Ms. Geller filed suit alleging violation of ADEA (Age Discrimination in Employment Act of 1967), 29 U.S.C. §§ 621, *et seq.* She also pointed, in particular, the "Sixth Step Policy."

Issue: Whether the school board's cost-cutting policy of hiring only teachers below a certain level of experience violates the Age Discrimination in Employment Act of 1967.

Holding: Yes, disparate impact was established. Statistics of high correlation between experience and membership in a protected age group, such as 40 to 65 years of age, rendered the application of the "Sixth Step Policy" discriminatory as a matter of law. *Geller,* 635 F.2d at 1033.

Reasoning:

Major Premise: Disparate impact may be established by a showing that a teacher was subjected to a facially neutral policy disproportionately disadvantaging her as a member of a protected class. *Id.* at 1032.

Minor Premise: Discriminatory impact may be evidenced by statistics that infer that the school board's selection method or selection criteria resulted in employment of a larger share of one group (such as teachers under 40 years of age) than of another group (such as teachers over 40). *See id.* at 1032–33.

Conclusion: Statistical evidence presented by Ms. Geller established disparate impact by showing that she was "subjected to a facially neutral policy disproportionately disadvantaging her as a member of a protected class." *Id.*

F. Discrimination against the Disabled

The Vocational Rehabilitation Act of 1973 prohibits discrimination against people with disabilities. Covered employers must make "reasonable accommodation" to the limitations of employees with disabilities who are otherwise qualified to do the job. The Americans with Disabilities Act of 1990 (ADA), considered by many to be the most sweeping anti-discrimination law since the Civil Rights Act of 1964, became effective on July 26, 1992. It provides civil rights protections to individuals with disabilities in private-sector employment, public services, public accommodations, transportation, and telecommunications.

In *Clark v. Shoreline School District No. 412*, 720 P.2d 793 (Wash. 1986), a visually disabled and hearing-impaired teacher's discharge was upheld by the Washington Supreme Court after substantial evidence showed that the disability affected his performance. The teacher experienced problems with student discipline, exhibited deficient professional preparation, failed to establish appropriate educational objectives, and generally jeopardized the welfare and safety of the students in his charge.

A teacher with AIDS claimed that his reassignment to an administrative position violated Section 504 of the Vocational Rehabilitation Act. The court upheld the teacher's motion for a preliminary injunction reinstating him to classroom duties. The court noted the overwhelming consensus of medical testimony, which revealed that the teacher posed no significant risk of spreading the disease. See *Chalk v. United States District Court*, 840 F.2d 701 (9th Cir. 1988).

VIII. TEACHER BARGAINING

The collective bargaining practices vary greatly from state to state. Some states have no statutes relating to collective bargaining; in fact, there are states that prohibit collective bargaining for public employees. On the contrary, there are states where there are extensive bargaining rights, including the right to strike. According to the National Education Association, about 70% of the states have laws that provide some form of collective bargaining for teachers. However, only eight states allow teachers to strike.

One issue that is often litigated is whether teachers who do not belong to the local union must pay compulsory union dues.

Lehnert v. Ferris Faculty Ass'n
500 U.S. 507, 111 S. Ct. 1950, 114 L. Ed. 2d 572 (1991)

Topic: Collection and Uses of Compulsory Union Dues

Facts: Michigan's Public Employment Relations Act provides that a duly selected union shall serve as the exclusive collective bargaining representative of public employees in a particular bargaining unit. The Act applies to faculty members of a public educational institution and permits a union and government employers to enter into a "union shop" arrangement under which employees within the bargaining unit who decline to become members are compelled to pay a "service fee" to the union.

Non-members of the union challenged the Act's agency-shop provision outlining permissible union uses of the "service fee." They claimed that such uses for purposes other than negotiating and administering the collective-bargaining agreement violated their rights under the First and Fourteenth Amendments.

Issue: Whether constitutional limitations exist upon the payment, required as a condition of employment, of dues by a nonmember to a union in the public sector.

Holding: Yes, in an agency shop or union shop, the expenses of a union's activities may be charged to nonmembers who object to such expenses under the following conditions: (1) chargeable activities must be "germane" to collective-bargaining activity; (2) charging dissenting nonmembers for such activities is justified by the government's policy interest in labor peace and avoiding "free-riders" who benefit from union efforts without paying for union services; and (3) charging dissenting nonmembers for such activities does not significantly add to the burdening of free speech that is inherent in the allowance of an agency or union shop. 500 U.S. at 516–18.

Reasoning:

Major Premise: To force employees to contribute, albeit indirectly, to their collective bargaining representative's promotion of a wide range of social, political, and ideological viewpoints implicates core concerns under the Federal Constitution's First Amendment. *Id.* at 516.

Minor Premise: Regarding union expenditures charged to dissenting nonmembers, not every charge that does not relate to a union activity is invalid under the First Amendment. *Id.* at 526.

Conclusion: Certain guidelines determine which activities a union constitutionally may charge to dissenting nonmembers. Chargeable activities must (1) be "germane" to collective-bargaining activity; (2) be justified by governmental interest in labor peace and avoiding "free riders"; and (3) not significantly add to the burdening of free speech that is inherent in an agency or union shop. *Id.* at 519.

Notes

In *Abood v. Detroit Board of Education,* 431 U.S. 209 (1977) and in *Chicago Teachers Union Local No. 1 v. Hudson,* 475 U.S. 292 (1986), the courts addressed fair procedures governing a union's collection of agency fees from nonmembers. In their decisions, the courts held that the Constitution requires (1) an adequate explanation of the basis for the fee; (2) a reasonably prompt opportunity to challenge the amount of the fee before an impartial decision maker; and (3) an escrow for the amounts reasonably in dispute while such a challenge is pending.

IX. POLITICAL ACTIVITIES

Four significant legal issues are involved when a public school employee becomes a candidate for public office or campaigns for other political candidates and issues. These issues are (1) the school employee's First Amendment rights of freedom of expression and association, (2) incompatibility of office provisions, (3) conflict-of-interest provisions, and (4) nepotism provisions.

A plethora of case law has established that a public school employee may not simultaneously hold a public office and his or her school employment if this is against (1) incompatibility of office provisions, (2) conflict of interest provisions, and (3) provisions providing for the tripartite separation of the divisions of government.

As far as campaigning for other political candidates and issues is concerned, public school employees have a First Amendment right to do so provided that these types of activities do not take place during school hours, do not take place in the classroom, do not interfere with the school employee's job performance, and if the employee does not use his or her school position to influence the outcome of the election.

Chapter Six

School Desegregation

In 1896, a Supreme Court decision established what has become known as the "separate but equal" doctrine regarding public facilities, including schools, used by African Americans. The **Plessy v. Ferguson** decision established a legal basis for segregating schools, thereby creating *de jure* (by law) segregation in the United States. Under this dual-school system approach, African-American students attended schools staffed by African American teachers, and Caucasian students attended schools staffed by Caucasian teachers. Separate but equal school systems were mostly found in the Southern states.

In 1954, the United States Supreme Court made the decision to reverse **Plessy** in **Brown v. Board of Education**. In this case, the Court ruled that in the field of public education, the doctrine of separate but equal "had no place." This landmark decision held that *de jure* segregation was unconstitutional. However, it did not address what would become an equally serious problem, *de facto* segregation.

The desegregation cases treated in this chapter give us an historical perspective. The evolution of the case law in this area is an interesting study. We will find that more than fifty years after **Brown**, segregation still persists.

I. HISTORICAL PERSPECTIVE

A. Doctrine of Separate But Equal

Plessy v. Ferguson
163 U.S. 537, 16 S. Ct. 1138, 41 L. Ed. 256 (1896)

Topic: Doctrine of Separate But Equal

Facts: The General Assembly of the State of Louisiana passed, in 1890, an act requiring "that all railway companies carrying passengers in their coaches in this state shall provide equal but separate accommodations for the white and colored races, by providing two or more passenger coaches for each passenger train, or by dividing the passenger coaches by a partition so as to secure separate accommodations . . . No person or persons shall be permitted to occupy seats in coaches other than the ones assigned to them, on account of the race they belong to." *Plessy*, 163 U.S. at 540. The Act imposed fines or imprisonment for violators.

Homer Adolph Plessy was "seven-eights Caucasian and one-eight African blood . . . the mixture of colored blood was not discernible in him." *Id*. at 541. Plessy took a seat in a coach where passengers of the white race were accommodated. He was ordered by the conductor to vacate the coach and take a seat in another coach assigned to persons of the colored race. Upon his refusal, he was arrested and jailed.

Issue: Whether the state statute providing for separate but equal railway accommodations for the white and colored races violates the Thirteenth Amendment of the Constitution abolishing slavery, and the Fourteenth Amendment, which prohibits certain restrictive legislation on the part of the states.

Holding: No, a statute that implies merely a legal distinction between the white and colored races has no tendency to destroy the legal equality of the two races, or re-establish a state of involuntary servitude. 163 U.S. at 543. A state statute requiring separate accommodations for white and colored persons on railroads does not violate the Thirteenth Amendment. *Id.* at 543.

Reasoning:

Major Premise: Where the civil and political rights of both races are equal, one cannot be inferior to the other. *Id.* at 551–52.

Minor Premise: "If one race be inferior to the other socially, the Constitution of the United States cannot put them upon the same plane." *Id.* at 552.

Conclusion: The Louisiana statute requiring separate accommodations for white and colored persons does not violate the Thirteenth Amendment or the Fourteenth Amendment.

Notes

After the Civil War, the Southern states adopted the so-called "Jim Crow" laws designed to separate the races. They required separate public facilities, such as toilets, water fountains, recreational facilities, and schools for African Americans and Caucasians. In 1927, the Court specifically extended **Plessy** to schools in *Gong Lum v. Rice,* 275 U.S. 78 (1927).

B. *De Jure* Segregation

Plessy was dealt a mortal blow by **Brown v. Board of Education**, but the groundwork for that decision was established in a number of earlier cases. In one of these cases, an African American law school applicant challenged a policy under which he had to attend an out-of-state law school because his home state did not have a "separate" law school for African Americans. The Court held that such an arrangement did not meet the "separate but equal" doctrine. See *Missouri ex rel. Gaines v. Canada,* 305 U.S. 337 (1938). In another decision, *Sweatt v. Painter,* 339 U.S. 629 (1950), the Court contended that "separate" law schools in Texas were not "equal" to those attended by Caucasians. In its decision, the Court not only compared tangible factors between racially segregated law schools but also such intangible factors as prestige, faculty reputation, and experience of the administration. Decisions such as *Gaines, Sweatt,* and others set the stage for a challenge to the *de jure* segregation practices in the public schools. In **Brown,** the Court decided that *de jure* segregation was a denial of the Fourteenth Amendment's guarantee of equal protection under the law.

Brown v. Bd. of Educ. of Topeka
347 U.S. 483, 74 S. Ct. 686, 98 L. Ed. 873 (1954)

Topic: Desegregation

Facts: Plaintiffs, African American children, were denied admission to state public schools attended by white children under state laws requiring or permitting segregation according to race.

There are findings that "the Negro and white schools involved have been equalized, or are being equalized, with respect to buildings, curricula, qualifications and salaries of teachers, and other 'tangible' factors." *Brown,* 347 U.S. at 492. However, the plaintiffs contend that "segregated public schools are not 'equal' and cannot be made 'equal,' and that hence they are deprived of the equal protection of the laws." *Id.* at 488.

Issue: Whether segregation in public education deprived the African-American children of the equal protection of the laws under the Fourteenth Amendment.

Holding: Yes, in the field of public education, the doctrine of "separate but equal" has no place. *Id*. at 495. Further, separate educational facilities are inherently unequal. *Id*. Therefore, by reason of segregation, plaintiff African American children are deprived of the equal protection of the laws guaranteed by the Fourteenth Amendment. *Id*.

Reasoning:

Major Premise: The Fourteenth Amendment guarantees equal protection of the laws.

Minor Premise: Racially separate facilities are inherently unequal.

Conclusion: Racially separate facilities violate the Fourteenth Amendment.

Notes

It should be emphasized that the consolidated opinion in **Brown** addressed *de jure* segregation the public schools. Consequently, **Brown** applied only to those states having government-imposed segregation at the time of the decision. It did not apply to *de facto* segregated schools outside of the South. Criticism on legalistic grounds focused on the fact that the Court relied on sociological evidence to establish the negative effect of segregation on African American students rather than relying on precedent.

C. Implementation of Brown I (Brown II)

Brown was a landmark case and its holding was responsible for the desegregation of public schools. However, the decision did not address the details or the timing of desegregation. In *Brown v. Board of Education of Topeka II,* 339 U.S. 294 (1955), the Supreme Court spoke to the timing with which desegregation should take place by declaring that it should take place "with all deliberate speed." The Court thought it was being specific, but the interpretation of "all deliberate speed" was to become problematic.

II. DESEGREGATION IN THE SOUTH

In **Brown II**, local school authorities were given the responsibility for devising an appropriate desegregation plan. The lower courts were to determine if these plans were sincere and effective. However, in the South, where there was considerable resistance to the decision, desegregation efforts were delayed and even circumvented.

As a result, the lower federal courts were inundated with desegregation cases where local authorities sometimes overtly refused to comply with the **Brown** decision. For example, Governor Orville Faubus of Arkansas received national attention when he stood on the high school steps in Little Rock and declared that no African American children could enter Little Rock High School. He actually called out the Arkansas national guard to enforce his decision. Ultimately, President Truman had the African American children escorted into Little Rock High School, thus complying with the Supreme Court's decision.

In Virginia, the compulsory-education laws were repealed and school attendance was made a matter of local option. Prince Edward County closed its schools, and private schools for whites only were operated in their places with state and county assistance. The Supreme Court rejected such a course in *Griffin v. County School Board of Prince Edward County,* 377 U.S. 218 (1964), by instructing the local district court to require the authorities to levy taxes, thereby raising funds to reopen and operate a nondiscriminatory public school system, such as those in other Virginia counties.

Another ploy to delay desegregation was the so-called freedom-of-choice plan. Under these plans, parents had the choice of determining which school their children would attend. The result was that all of the whites parents chose one school, and the African American parents were intimidated into choosing another school.

A. Freedom of Choice Plans

Green v. County Sch. Bd. of New Kent County
391 U.S. 430, 88 S. Ct. 1689, 20 L. Ed. 2d 716 (1968)

Topic: Freedom of Choice Plans

Facts: New Kent County has only two schools, the New Kent school on the east side and the George W. Watkins school on the west side. The School Board operates one white combined elementary and high school (New Kent) and one Negro combined elementary and high school (George W. Watkins). *Green*, 391 U.S. 432.

To comply with the mandate of *Brown v. Board of Education*, and in order to remain eligible for federal financial aid, the School Board adopted a "freedom-of-choice" plan for desegregating the schools. *Id.* Under this plan, students may annually choose between the New Kent and Watkins schools and students not making a choice are assigned to the school previously attended. *Id.* at 434. In the three years the plan was in operation, not a single white child had chosen to attend Watkins school, and although a number of Negro children had enrolled in New Kent school, 85% of the Negro children in the system still attended the Negro Watkins school. *Id.* at 441.

Issue: Whether the School Board's adoption of the "freedom-of-choice" plan that allows a student to choose his own public school constitutes adequate compliance with the Board's responsibility "to achieve a system of determining admission to the public schools on a non-racial basis" under *Brown II*.

Holding: No, rather than dismantling the dual system, the "freedom-of-choice" plan has burdened the children and their parents with the responsibility placed by Brown II on the School Board. 391 U.S. 441–42. In addition, the plan could not be accepted as a sufficient step to "effectuate a transition" to a unitary, nonracial system. *Id.* at 441. Therefore, the School Board is required to fashion steps that promise realistic and immediate conversion to a system without a "white school" and a "negro school," but just schools. *Id.* at 442.

Reasoning:

Major Premise: The School Board was required to bear the burden of providing a plan that will realistically and expediently create a "unitary, non-racial system." *Id.* at 440.

Minor Premise: If there are reasonably available ways that promise speedier and more effective conversion to a unitary, nonracial school system, "freedom-of-choice" must be held unacceptable. *Id.* at 441.

Conclusion: Because the school system remains a dual system, the "freedom-of-choice" plan was ineffective as a tool of desegregation. *Id.* Therefore, the Board must be required to formulate a new plan that would promise realistic and immediate conversion to a system without a "white school" and a "negro school," but just schools. *Id.* at 442.

Notes

In **Green**, the Court declared that "all deliberate speed" was now interpreted as "immediately." This immediacy was reinforced in *Alexander v. Holmes County Board of Education*, 396 U.S. 19 (1969).

B. Busing for Desegregation

Swann v. Charlotte–Mecklenburg Bd. of Educ.
402 U.S. 1, 91 S. Ct. 1267, 28 L. Ed. 2d 554 (1971)

Topic: School Desegregation and Busing

Facts: The Charlotte–Mecklenburg school system encompasses the city of Charlotte and surrounding Mecklenburg County, North Carolina. The school system is the 43rd largest in the United States. During the 1968–1969 school year, the system served more than 84,000 students in 107 schools.

Approximately 71% of the students were white and 29% Negro. As of June 1969, there were about 24,000 Negro students in the school system, of which 21,000 attended schools within the city of Charlotte. Two-thirds of the 21,000, or about 14,000 Negro students, attended 21 schools that were either totally Negro or more than 99% Negro.

The school system failed to achieve the unitary school system mandated by *Green v. County Sch. Bd. of New Kent County*, 391 U.S. 430, 88 S. Ct. 1689, 20 L. Ed. 2d 716 (1968).

Issues: What are the duties of school authorities and the scope of powers of federal courts under the Supreme Court's mandates to eliminate racially separate public schools established and maintained by state action?

1. What extent racial balance or racial quotas may be used as an implement in a remedial order to correct a previously segregated system?
2. Whether every all-Negro and all-white school must be eliminated as an indispensable part of a remedial process of desegregation.
3. What limits are, if any, on the rearrangement of school districts and attendance zones, as a remedial measure?
4. What limits are, if any, on the use of transportation facilities to correct state-enforced racial school segregation?

Holding: If school authorities fail in their affirmative obligations in eliminating from the public schools "all vestiges of state-imposed segregation," the scope of a district court's equitable power to remedy past wrongs is broad. *Swann*, 402 U.S. at 15.

1. Limited use of mathematical ratios is within the equitable remedial discretion of the District Court. 402 U.S. at 25.
2. The existence of some small number of one-race schools within a district is not in and of itself the mark of a system that still practices segregation by law. *Id.* at 26.
3. The pairing and grouping of noncontiguous school zones is a permissible tool and such action is to be considered in light of the objectives sought. *Id.* at 28.
4. The District Court's order requiring additional busing of elementary and secondary school students as a means of school desegregation were within the court's power to provide equitable relief. *Id.* at 30.

Reasoning:

Major Premise: Dual school systems violates the Fourteenth Amendment. School authorities are "clearly charged with the affirmative duty to take whatever steps might be necessary to convert to a unitary system in which racial discrimination will be eliminated root and branch." *Id.* at 15.

Minor Premise: If school authorities fail in their affirmative obligations to eliminate racially segregated schools, judicial authority may be invoked. *Id.*

Conclusion: The scope of a District Court's equitable powers to remedy past wrongs is broad. *Id.*

Notes

In **Swann**, the Court once again demonstrated its fervor in bringing about the desegregation of public schools. The holding contended that the dismantling of the dual school system could be accomplished by assigning teachers so as to achieve a particular degree of faculty desegregation; ensuring that future school construction and abandonment would not perpetuate or reestablish a dual system; scrutinizing one-race schools to ensure that the racial composition did not result from present or past discriminatory action; altering attendance zones and employing pairing and grouping of noncontiguous zones to counteract past segregation; and although not requiring it, employing bus transportation as a constitutionally permissible method of dismantling the dual system.

III. DESEGREGATION IN NON-SOUTHERN STATES

The desegregation of the public schools in the Southern states overshadowed similar efforts in the Northern states for about twenty years after the **Brown** decision. One of the reasons that it took so long to address the obvious segregation issue in Northern and Western public schools was the Supreme Court's requirement that *de jure* segregation be present for jurisdiction to take place. It was difficult to demonstrate that these school districts intentionally segregated the schools.

Perhaps the most significant force contributing to Northern and Western segregation was housing patterns. Such *de facto* segregation was often based on busing patterns that allegedly were not the result of direct state action. Since the Supreme Court had not considered *de facto* segregation a violation of **Brown I**, school districts that were segregated on that basis were not immediately challenged. However, one of the claims made by integrationists was that the non-Southern states engaged in a form of *de jure* segregation, also.

A. Inter-district Integration

Milliken v. Bradley
418 U.S. 717, 94 S. Ct. 3112, 41 L. Ed. 2d 1069 (1974)

Topic: Multi-District Desegregation Plan

Facts: A class-action suit was brought alleging that the Detroit public school system is racially segregated as a result of the official policies and actions of state and local officials. The suit also seeks implementation of a plan to eliminate the segregation and establish a unitary nonracial school system.

Evidence of *de jure* segregation exists in the Detroit Area School District, which is predominantly black. On the other hand, the 85 outlying suburban districts were not parties to the class-action suit and there was no claim that they had committed constitutional violations.

The District Court ordered state officials to submit desegregation plans encompassing the three-county metropolitan area including 53 of the 85 suburban school districts.

Issue: Whether a federal court may impose a multi-district remedy for a single district's *de jure* segregation.

Holding: No, absent an inter-district violation, there is no basis for an inter-district remedy. *Milliken*, 418 U.S. at 752. A federal court may not impose a multi-district remedy for a single-district *de jure* school desegregation, where there is no finding that (1) the other school districts failed to operate unitary school system or committed acts that effected segregation within the other districts, and (2) the school district's boundary lines were established for the purpose of fostering racial segregation.

Reasoning:

Major Premise: Desegregation, in the sense of dismantling a dual school system, does not require any particular racial balance in school, grade, or classroom. *Id*. at 740–41.

Minor Premise: In school desegregation cases, a federal remedial power may be exercised "only on the basis of a constitutional violation" and, "the nature of the violation determines the scope of the remedy." *Id*. at 738.

Conclusion: The constitutional right of Negro students is to attend a unitary school system in their district. *Id*. at 746. Unless the state drew the district lines in a discriminatory fashion or arranged for white students to attend schools in adjacent districts, the state is under no constitutional duty to make provisions for the Negro students to do so. *Id*. at 746–47. Therefore, the mere existence of a dual system in the school district cannot be made the basis for ordering cross-district transportation of students. *Id*. at 747.

Notes

Many observers consider **Milliken** to be the end of the Supreme Court's unwavering support of desegregation. As we have seen in other instances, over time the courts limit the effects of the original holdings.

B. De Jure Segregation in Non-Southern States

In the mid-seventies, school desegregation cases shifted from the South to the Northern and Western urban areas. In decisions involving Dayton and Columbus, Ohio, the Supreme Court continued to rely on *de jure* segregation, but did so in non-Southern states. The court maintained that if racially segregated dual school systems were operated at the time of **Brown** in 1954, boards of education had an "affirmative duty" not to engage in actions that would have impeded the desegregation process. Additionally, in a decision involving Denver, Colorado, the Court held that

> . . . a finding of intentionally segregative school board action in a meaningful portion of a school system, as in this case, creates a presumption that other segregated schooling within the system is not adventitious. It establishes, in other words, a prima facie case of unlawful segregative design on the part of school authorities, and shifts to those authorities the burden of proving that other segregated schools within the system are not also the result of intentionally segregative action. [*Keyes v. School District No. 1*, 413 U.S. 189, 208 (1973)].

Keyes was the first case of a school district without a history of *de jure* segregation to come before the Supreme Court.

Columbus Bd. of Educ. v. Penick
443 U.S. 449, 99 S. Ct. 2941, 61 L. Ed. 2d 666 (1979)

Topic: Intentional Segregative Action

Facts: The public school system of Columbus, Ohio, is highly segregated by race. In 1976, the public school system had 96,000 students attending 172 schools. About 32% of the students were black, however, approximately 70% of the students attended schools that were at least 80% black or 80% white. Half of the schools were 90% black or 90% white.

A class-action suit was brought by fourteen named students against the Columbus Board of Education. The suit charged that the defendants "had pursued and were pursuing a course of conduct having the purpose and effect of causing and perpetuating segregation in the public schools, contrary to the Fourteenth Amendment." *Penick*, 443 U.S. at 452.

The District Court enjoined the Board of Education from continuing to discriminate on the basis of race in operating the public school system. In addition, the Board was ordered to submit a system-wide desegregation plan.

Issue: Whether the District Court's findings of fact were clearly erroneous and whether the Court misunderstood or misapplied the Fourteenth Amendment and relevant cases construing it.

Holding: No, the conduct of the Columbus Board of Education was animated by an unconstitutional, segregative purpose. 443 U.S. at 455. The segregative impact was substantially system-wide to warrant the remedy ordered by the District Court. *Id.* Proof of purposeful and effective maintenance of separate black schools in a substantial part of the school system provides sufficient basis for the inference of a system-wide discriminatory intent, and contrary proof by the Board was absent. *Id.* at 458.

Reasoning:

Major Premise: The constitutional duty to eliminate a dual school system resulting from local segregative acts and policies is not a lesser duty than the constitutional duty to eliminate dual school systems ordained by law. *Id.* at 457 n.5.

Minor Premise: Proof of purposeful and effective maintenance of a body of separate black schools in a substantial part of the public school system is itself a prima facie proof of a dual school system. *Id.* at 458.

Conclusion: The conduct of the Columbus Board of Education at the time of trial and before not only was animated by an unconstitutional, segregative purpose, but also had current, segregative impact that was substantially system-wide to warrant the remedy ordered by the District Court. *Id.* at 455.

C. Release from Court Order

After school systems across the country were placed under court order to desegregate, the next logical question was when they would be released from the court order? Two United States Supreme Court rulings in the early 1990s address this issue. In **Board of Education of Oklahoma City Public Schools v. Dowell**, the court reveals its definition of the term "unitary," and that court supervision was intended to be a temporary measure. **Freeman v. Pitts** held that federal district courts have the discretion to withdraw their supervision over formerly segregated school systems incrementally and are not responsible for segregation based on demographic changes in student population after desegregation takes place.

Board of Educ. of Oklahoma City v. Dowell
498 U.S. 237, 111 S. Ct. 630, 112 L. Ed. 2d 715 (1991)

Topic: Release from Court-Ordered School Desegregation

Facts: Several black students and their parents brought suit in 1961 against the Board of Education of Oklahoma City seeking to end alleged, *de jure* segregation of the city's public schools. In 1972, the District Court ordered the adoption of a desegregation plan that includes mandatory student assignments to specified schools and grades, and school busing.

Five years later, in 1977, the District Court found that (1) the desegregation plan had worked; (2) substantial compliance with the constitutional requirements had been achieved; and (3) a "unitary" school system had been accomplished.

After several proceedings, the Court of Appeals reversed, expressed the view that the desegregation decree remains in effect until the school district can show a "grievous wrong" evoked by new and unforeseen conditions.

Issue: Whether the Court of Appeal's test for dissolving a desegregation decree is more stringent than is required either by the Supreme Court's decisions dealing with injunctions or by the Equal Protection Clause of the Fourteenth Amendment.

Holding: Yes. The District Court's finding is a finding that the purposes of the desegregation litigation have been fully achieved and is thus sufficient to justify dissolution of the desegregation decree. 498 U.S. at 247. There is no additional requirement for the school board to show a "grievous wrong" evoked by new and unforeseen conditions. *Id*. The test adopted by the Court of Appeals would condemn a school district to judicial tutelage for the indefinite future. *Id*. at 249.

Reasoning:

Major Premise: To decide whether the vestiges of *de jure* segregation of public schools have been eliminated, the District Court should look at not only school assignments, but also "to every facet of school operations—faculty, staff, transportation, extracurricular activities, and facilities." *Id*. at 250.

Minor Premise: Based on its finding, the District Court found that the Oklahoma City School District was in compliance with the Equal Protection Clause of the Fourteenth Amendment, and it was unlikely that the Board would return to its former ways. *Id*. at 247.

Conclusion: The purpose of the desegregation litigation had been fully achieved. *Id*. "Dissolving a desegregation decree after the local authorities have operated in compliance with it for a reasonable period of time properly recognizes that 'necessary concern for the important values of local control of public school systems dictates that a federal court's regulatory control of such systems not extend beyond the time required to remedy the effects of past intentional discrimination.'" *Id*. at 248.

Freeman v. Pitts
503 U.S. 467, 112 S. Ct. 1430, 118 L. Ed. 2d 108 (1992)

Topic: Release from Court-Ordered School Desegregation

Facts: The DeKalb County School System (DCSS), pursuant to a court-ordered desegregation decree, has been subject to the supervision and jurisdiction of the United States District Court since 1969. DCSS was ordered to dismantle its dual school system according to the factors identified in *Green v. County Sch. Bd. of New Kent County*, 391 U.S. 430, 88 S. Ct. 1689, 20 L. Ed. 2d 716 (1968). Green identified six factors in order to achieve unitary status: student assignments, transportation, physical facilities, extracurricular activities, faculty assignments, and resource allocation.

In 1986, the District Court ruled DCSS had achieved a unitary status with respect to four of the six factors identified in *Green*, and the Court would relinquish remedial control as to those aspects of the system in which unitary status had been achieved. However, the Court refused to dismiss the case because it found that DCSS was not unitary with respect to the two remaining factors: faculty assignments and resource allocation.

Accordingly, the District Court retained supervisory authority only for those aspects of the school system in which the district was not in full compliance. The Court of Appeals reversed and held that a district court should retain full remedial authority over a school system until it achieves unitary status in all *Green* categories.

Issue: Whether a district court may relinquish its supervision and control over those aspects of a school system in which there has been compliance with a desegregation decree if other aspects of the system remain in noncompliance.

Holding: Yes, in the course of supervising desegregation plans, federal courts have the authority to relinquish supervision and control of school districts in incremental stages, before full compliance has been achieved in every area of school operations. *Freeman*, 503 U.S. 490.

Reasoning:

Major Premise: Local autonomy of school districts is a vital national tradition. *Id.* (Citing *Dayton v. Bd. of Educ. v. Brinkman*, 433 U.S. 406, 410 (1977).)

Minor Premise: One of the prerequisites to relinquishment of judicial control, in whole or in part, is that a school district has demonstrated its commitment to a course of action that gives full respect to the equal protection guarantees of the Constitution. *Id.*

Conclusion: In the course of supervising desegregation plans, federal courts have the authority to relinquish supervision and control of school districts in incremental stages. *Id.*

D. Mandating Taxes for Desegregation

The expenses of court-ordered desegregation are often greater than taxpayers are willing to bear. The United States Supreme Court addressed the issue of court-mandated tax increases to fund desegregation efforts in **Missouri v. Jenkins**.

Missouri v. Jenkins
495 U.S. 33, 110 S. Ct. 1651, 109 L. Ed. 2d 31 (1990)

Topic: Mandating a Tax Increase to Fund Desegregation

Facts: A group of Kansas City, Missouri, School District (KCMSD) students are the plaintiffs in a suit involving several defendants, including the State of Missouri and KCMSD. The suit alleged that the defendants had operated a racially segregated public school system. In a series of decisions, the District Court ordered certain remedies deemed necessary to eliminate vestiges of segregation, and the financing deemed necessary to implement those remedies.

   However, the District Court eventually concluded that the KCMSD had exhausted all available means of raising additional revenue to pay for KCMSD's share of the cost of the remedy. Consequently, the District Court ordered the "KCMSD property tax levy" increased, from $2.05 to $4.00 per $100 of assessed valuation through the 1991–1992 fiscal year, to fund the desegregation remedy.

Issue: Whether the District Court lacked the power to raise local property taxes to fund a court-imposed desegregation remedies.

Holding: Yes, a Federal District Court may not directly impose property tax increase to fund a desegregation remedy, but it may have authority to order the school district to levy such taxes. *See Jenkins*, 495 U.S. at 37, 51.

Reasoning:

Major Premise: Authorizing and directing local government institutions to devise and implement remedies not only protects the function of those institutions but also places the responsibility for solutions to the problems of segregation upon those who have themselves created the problems. 495 U.S. at 51.

Minor Premise: Before a federal court may impose a tax increase to fund a desegregation remedy, it must assure itself that no permissible alternative would have accomplished the task. *Id.*

Conclusion: The District Court could have authorized or required KCMSD to levy property taxes at a rate adequate to fund the desegregation remedy, therefore the Court abused its discretion in directly imposing the property tax increase. *Id.* at 51–52.

IV. EPILOGUE

The **Brown** decision was truly monumental not only for education, but also in the areas of public accommodation, housing, and voting. Equality for African Americans before the law became a reality. However, almost fifty years after the decision, the advances that were hoped for have not become a part of the American culture. There are even doubts now about the effectiveness of busing as a desirable means of achieving desegregation. Some parents would rather leave their children in a segregated school than have them bused to another area of the city for desegregation purposes. Court-ordered numerical quotas have also been contested. And the white flight that often occurs in a desegregation situation also exacerbates the situation.

Desegregation has been successful in the South, were now only 26% of the minority students attend one-race schools. Outside of the South, however, the results have been mixed, at best. Almost two-thirds of the African American children attend schools populated mostly by their own race. Inner city schools have become so universally populated with minority students that the term "minority" becomes a misnomer. As long as educational achievement remained so closely associated with socio-economic status, however, the effort to group young people heterogeneously according to race and economic status is a worthwhile endeavor.

Chapter Seven

School Finance Issues

This chapter deals with the issue of financial equity in the state funding of schools and with the issue of parental choice in schooling. Both of these issues are topical. The funding issue has been litigated frequently; however, the school choice issue is still evolving, but the Supreme Court has decided in a 5-4 decision that tuition vouchers do not violate the First Amendment of the Constitution.

I. SCHOOL FINANCE REFORM

A. Background

The issue of educational funding has been litigated with the plaintiffs in these cases claiming that many state methods of financing public education were unconstitutional because they violated the Equal Protection Clause for certain classes of people. Reliance on local revenue to support a large portion of the total public school budget, it was alleged, was unfair because of the disparity in taxable wealth among local school systems. Because the property tax is the most commonly used local school tax, many school finance experts have defined school system wealth as the ratio of taxable property divided by the number of students. Consequently, a "wealthy" school system would achieve such status by having much valuable taxable property, such as factories, utilities, or natural resources, and few children to educate. Conversely, a "poor" school system would have little valuable property and many children to educate. A school system composed largely of trailer parks, where each trailer contained several school-age children, would be an example of a poor system.

To place the funding situation in perspective, on a national basis, local revenue has made up approximately 47% of the total revenue for elementary and secondary schools in school districts, whereas state revenue made up approximately 47% and federal revenue 6%.

Those who maintain that a state's method of financing the public schools is unfair often argue that wealthy school systems can raise large amounts of money with lower tax rates than can poor systems. It is alleged that allowing this situation under a state-authorized method of financing public education is unfair to both taxpayers and the recipients of school services in poor systems. Because education is a responsibility of the state, school finance reformers allege that a state's allowing a school financing system in which such disparities operate in favor of wealthy school systems denies equality of educational opportunity to those students in poorer school systems. The issue that has received the greatest court attention addressed the alleged inequality of educational opportunity resulting from statewide school finance systems that make educational funding a function of district property wealth.

B. Early Court Cases

In *McInnis v. Shapiro,* 293 F.Supp. 427 (Ill. 1968), the Illinois method of financing public education was described by plaintiffs as being particularly inequitable because it permitted wide variations in expenditures per student and did not apportion funds according to the educational needs of students. In rejecting this contention, the court declared that the controversy was essentially non-justifiable because of a lack of judicially manageable standards. The court contended that equal expenditures per student were inappropriate as a standard and that courts were ill prepared to devise an equitable financing plan for the public schools. A virtually indistinguishable case, *Burruss v. Wilkerson,* 310 F. Supp. 572 (Va. 1969), essentially reached the same conclusion as *McInnis.*

C. Fiscal Neutrality

The holdings in the *McInnis* and *Burruss* cases did not dissuade the legal challenges to the school funding formulae in the various states. A California case, *Serrano v. Priest,* 487 P.2d 1241 (Cal. 1971), provided the court with a judicially manageable standard, which had been missing in earlier cases. In this case, the plaintiffs attempted to demonstrate that the California method of financing public education allowed substantial disparities among the various school districts in the amount of revenue available for education, thereby denying students equal protection of the laws under both the United States and California constitutions.

In addition, the plaintiffs alleged that under this funding system, parents were required to pay taxes at a higher rate than taxpayers in many other districts in order to provide the same or lesser education opportunities for their children. In its decision, the California Supreme Court established that education was a constitutionally protected fundamental interest and that "wealth" was a "suspect classification." When a fundamental interest or suspect classification is involved, the court contended, the state must establish not only that it has a compelling interest that justifies the law, but also that the distinctions drawn by the law are necessary to further its purpose. Employing this line of reasoning places the burden of proof on the state. This case also established the standard to determine whether or not a school-funding plan was constitutional. Under this standard, which the court called "fiscal neutrality," the quality of a child's education could not be based on the wealth of the child's local school district but rather had to be based on the wealth of the state as a whole. This provided the court with a judicially manageable standard, in contrast to the "needs" standard in earlier cases, as the court merely had to reject the present financing plan as unconstitutional, thereby placing the burden of adopting a constitutionally acceptable finance plan with the state.

Suits were filed in both state and federal courts in more than three dozen states after the *Serrano* decision. One of these cases, **San Antonio Independent School District v. Rodriguez**, provided the United States Supreme Court with an opportunity to address this issue.

San Antonio Indep. Sch. Dist. v. Rodriguez
411 U.S. 1, 93 S. Ct. 1278, 36 L. Ed. 2d 16 (1973)

Topic: Fiscal Neutrality

Facts: Mexican American parents brought a class action suit on behalf of school children throughout the state who are members of minority groups or who are poor and reside in school districts having a low property tax base. The plaintiffs challenged the financing of public elementary and secondary schools in Texas.

Approximately one-half of the school revenues are derived from a state-funded program designed to provide a basic minimum education in every school. School districts supplement their funding with an ad valorem tax on property within its jurisdiction. Plaintiffs claim that the Texas system's reliance on local property taxation favors the more affluent and violates equal protection requirements. The plaintiffs contend that substantial inter-district disparities in per-pupil expenditures resulted from differences in the value of assessable property among the districts.

Issue: Whether the Texas system of financing public education operates to the disadvantage of some suspect class or impinges upon a fundamental right explicitly or implicitly protected by the Constitution, thus requiring strict judicial scrutiny.

Holding: No, the Texas system does not violate the Equal Protection Clause of the Fourteenth Amendment because the system bears a rational relationship to a legitimate state purpose, particularly in view of the Court's traditional deference to state legislatures in the areas of fiscal and educational policies and local taxation. 411 U.S. at 40–41, 55. There was no showing that any definable category of "poor" persons was discriminated against, that any child was suffering an absolute deprivation of public education, or that there was any comparative discrimination based on relative family income within the districts. *Id.* at 25, 28.

Reasoning:

Major Premise: Education is not among the rights afforded explicit or implicit protection under the Federal Constitution. 411 U.S. at 35.

Minor Premise: The traditional standard of review of state action under the equal protection clause of the Fourteenth Amendment—requiring that the state's action be shown to bear some rational relationship to a legitimate state purpose—is appropriate for application by the United States Supreme Court in reviewing a state's statutory system for financing public education. *Id.* at 40–41.

Conclusion: The Texas system does not violate the Equal Protection Clause of the Fourteenth Amendment because the system bears a rational relationship to a legitimate state purpose. *Id.* at 55.

Notes

In addition to upholding the constitutionality of the Texas method of financing public schools, the Court held that education was not a fundamental interest requiring strict scrutiny under the Equal Protection Clause. The Court also concluded that school finance reform should flow from state legislative processes.

D. Post-Rodriguez Litigation

Rodriguez essentially eliminated the federal courts as a venue for settling school finance issues. Consequently, the state courts became the forum for these debates. To date, the highest courts in more than a dozen states have concluded that the state's methods of financing public education did not violate state constitutional guarantees. Many of these decisions espoused the legal rationale enunciated in **Rodriguez**. They agreed that education was unquestionably an important property right and an important government concern. However, this did not automatically entitle public education to a classification as a fundamental right that would trigger a higher standard of judicial review for purposes of equal protection analysis. Public education in these cases was viewed as merely another public service battling for scarce resources in the political arena.

On the other hand, decisions by the highest courts in more than a dozen states have held that statutes determining state funding formulae were unconstitutional. Most decisions in other states ordered legislative restructuring of the basic formula for the distribution of state funds or the receipt of local revenues in order to eliminate or reduce local wealth disparity as a factor influencing expenditure variation among school districts or their ability to provide an adequate education. However, the most pervasive theme threading through these decisions was the courts' recognition of the irrationality of the contested finance schemes. The judicial battles regarding this issue continue.

Rose v. The Council for Better Education is typical of such cases.

Rose v. Council for Better Educ., Inc.
790 S.W.2d 186 (Ky. 1989)

Topic: School Finance

Facts: Council for Better Education, Inc. ("Council"), a non-profit Kentucky corporation, has a membership of sixty-six local school districts in the state. 790 S.W.2d at 190. Together with the Boards of Education of the Dayton and Harlan Independent School Districts, local school districts and 22 public school students, Council brought suit challenging the constitutionality of Kentucky's common school system. *Id.*

The defendants were the Governor, the Superintendent of Public Instruction, the State Treasurer, the President Pro Tempore of the Senate, the Speaker of the House of Representatives, and the State Board of Education and its individual members. *Id.*

The Kentucky Constitution set forth the following:

"General Assembly to provide for school system—The General Assembly shall, by appropriate legislation, provide for an *efficient* system of common schools throughout the state. Ky. Const. Sec. 183."

Council for Better Educ., Inc., 790 S.W.2d at 205 (Emphasis added).

The evidence presented at trial was "a virtual concession that Kentucky's system of common schools is underfunded and inadequate; is fraught with inequalities and inequities throughout the 177 local school districts; is ranked nationally in the lower 20–25% in virtually every category that is used to evaluate educational performance; and is not uniform among the districts in educational opportunities." *Id.* at 197.

Issue: Whether evidence supports the conclusion that the Kentucky system of common schools is not efficient, and therefore in violation of the Kentucky Constitution.

Holding: Yes, to be "efficient," the school system (1) must be adequately funded to achieve its goals; (2) must be substantially uniform throughout the state; and (3) each child must be provided with an equal opportunity to have an adequate education. *Id.* at 211. The current common school system did not satisfy the constitutional requirement that the General Assembly provide an efficient system of common schools throughout the state. *Id.* at 214.

Reasoning:

Major Premise: A child's right to an adequate education is a fundamental one under the Kentucky Constitution. 790 S.W.2d at 212.

Minor Premise: To fulfill the constitutional mandate that a system of common schools be provided throughout the entire state, the General Assembly had an obligation to provide an "efficient" common school system. *Id.* at 205.

Conclusion: Kentucky's entire system of common schools is inefficient, therefore unconstitutional. *Id.* at 215.

Notes

The **Rose** decision departed significantly from previous school finance decisions. It not only broadened the scope of court examination of related school finance issues, but also ordered an unprecedented restructuring of the state's entire educational system.

II. EDUCATIONAL CHOICE

School choice has become a topical and controversial subject in the contemporary world of education. Various attempts have been made to compensate for the alleged underachievement of today's public schools by offering parents and students state-supported alternatives to public education. What follows is a brief description of the various educational choice plans and the possible legal implications that would accompany implementation of these plans.

A. Choice Plans

The proponents of educational choice claim that the public schools are inefficient and ineffective in providing students with a thorough and efficient education. These educational choice advocates have attempted to provide educational reforms that are seemingly both educationally sound and politically attractive. One of the highly touted reforms, educational choice plans, provide for increased consumer selection of education services at public expense. To date, variations of choice plans have been enacted by several state legislatures. Opponents see choice plans as a direct challenge to the egalitarian notion that the bright, average, disabled, minority groups, Caucasian, and economically advantaged and disadvantaged all attend the same public school. Its proponents argue that bringing a concept like consumer choice to education will break the alleged monolithic advantage that public schools presently hold and introduce much needed competition.

1. Public School Inter-District and Intra-District Open Enrollment

Under these notions, students would be allowed to attend the school of their choice in their own school district or any district in the state, provided there was room at that school and that their attendance did not create segregation along racial lines. Generally, federal and state monies would follow the student. Minnesota has been the acknowledged leader in this form of choice, passing a law that allows families to send their children outside their district so long as the receiving school district has room and desegregation efforts are not jeopardized.

2. Inter-District Specialized Schools and Plans

The larger school districts in the country have experimented with plans that provide students with a choice of attending a school other than the one in their attendance zone. These plans, which often incorporate magnet schools, are put into place to effect desegregation, retain students who are contemplating dropping out of school, or offer specialized programs for academically advantaged students.

Magnet schools emphasize a particular educational feature such as mathematics, fine arts, or "back to basics." These schools have been considered a valuable tool in those school systems attempting to implement a desegregation policy. Unfortunately, their feasibility is limited to relatively large school districts.

Minischools, "houses," or schools within schools, are variants of the magnet school and attempt to provide educational alternatives within a particular school site. These alternatives are often seen in large schools systems that have been depicted as being bureaucratic and insensitive to individuals students' needs.

3. Voucher Plans

The concept of an educational voucher was first proposed by the Nobel Laureate economist, Milton Friedman, as a solution to what he perceived to be defects in the public school system. It was designed to give parents greater control of their children's schooling and to provide poor parents an opportunity for nonpublic school education. The original idea called for parents to receive a voucher redeemable for a specified sum per child per year if spent on approved educational services. The role of government would be confined to ensuring that schools met minimum standards. The voucher could be redeemed at any approved school, public or private, thereby providing parents with a measure of choice. The operation of several forces appears to be the reason for vouchers not gaining wider acceptance. These include: a fear that the public schools would become the dumping ground for students at risk; separation of church and state issues; issues surrounding desegregation and the education of students with disabilities; and the insecurity for teachers concerning their jobs. Despite these fears, several cities, including Milwaukee, are experimenting with a variety of voucher plans. A number of states, and even the federal government, have seriously contemplated such plans.

4. Charter Schools

Charter schools allow entities other than school boards to establish publicly funded schools. The theory behind such schools is to allow individuals or groups with innovative educational ideas to put them into practice without being unduly hampered by local or state bureaucracies and teacher unions. To date, various forms of charter school legislation have been passed in Arizona, California, Colorado, Connecticut, Georgia, Kansas, Massachusetts, Michigan, Minnesota, New Mexico, Pennsylvania, and Wisconsin.

5. Tuition Tax Credits

Although not always labeled as a choice plan, providing tuition tax credits for parents of school age children is designed to ease the financial burden of nonpublic school attendance. Under such plans, parents are allowed to claim a state income tax deduction from gross income on their state income tax returns for certain educational expenses incurred at either public or private schools. Prior to the Supreme Court's decision upholding a Minnesota tax deduction plan in *Muellar v. Allen*, 463 U.S. 388 (1983), courts had not upheld such plans, primarily because of separation of church and state issues.

B. Legal Implications

Choice plans are susceptible to a number of legal challenges. However, speculation surrounding the outcome of such litigation should be tempered by the recognition of the Supreme Court's strong proclivity to uphold nondiscriminatory state legislative action. Separation of church and state issues will undoubtedly arise if it appears that public funds, through the use of an educational voucher, will aid religious schools. As we have seen, the Supreme Court has shown considerable interest in this issue. The presently employed *Lemon* test establishes that a challenged statute must first have a secular legislative purpose; second, its primary effect must be one that neither advances nor inhibits religion; and third, it must not foster an excessive government entanglement with religion. Courts will have to determine whether a challenged plan violates any or all of these three prongs or the coercion test enunciate in *Lee v. Weisman*. Complicating the issue further would be the matter of a religious school's acceptance of voucher students if the school had rigid policies relating to the proselytizing of its beliefs. Only the future will tell as to how educational vouchers and other types of choice plans fare in the courts. However, the Supreme Court has recently adjudicated a case, *Zelman v. Simmons-Harris* (2002), in favor of the constitutionality of tuition vouchers. The Supreme Court may have been influenced by the rationale used in the *Jackson v. Benson case.*

Jackson v. Benson
No. 97-0270 (Wis. June 10, 1998)

Topic: Aid to Nonpublic Schools; Private School Voucher Program

Facts: Originally enacted by the Wisconsin legislature in 1989 and amended in 1995, the voucher program provides state aid to low-income parents of students in the Milwaukee public school system. The voucher program is called the Milwaukee Parental Choice Program (MPCP).

Pupils are eligible under the MPCP if they reside in Milwaukee, attend public schools (or private schools in grades K–3), and meet the income requirements. Beneficiaries are eligible for an equal share of per-pupil public aid regardless of the school they choose to attend. The MPCP gives participating parents the choice to send their children to a neighborhood public school, a different public school within the district, a specialized public school, a private nonsectarian school, or a private sectarian school. The State provides the aid by individual checks made payable to the parents of each pupil attending a private school under the program. Each check is then sent to the parents' choice of schools and can be cashed only for the cost of the student's tuition.

Participating private schools are subject to routine performance, reporting, and auditing requirements, as well as to applicable nondiscrimination, health, and safety obligations. The State Superintendent, as part of his existing duties, already monitors the quality of education at all sectarian private schools.

Issue: Whether the MPCP, by providing state aid for the benefit of religious private schools, violated the Establishment Clause of the First Amendment of the United States Constitution.

Holding: No, the MPCP's authorization of financial aid vouchers on the basis of religion-neutral eligibility criteria for parents who may choose to send children to either sectarian or nonsectarian private schools does not violate the Establishment Clause of the First Amendment.

Reasoning:

Major Premise: The Establishment Clause prohibits state governments from passing laws that either have the purpose or effect of advancing or inhibiting religion.

Minor Premise: A statute does not violate the Establishment Clause if (1) it has a secular purpose, (2) it will not have the primary effect of advancing religion, and (3) it will not lead to excessive entanglement between the state and participating sectarian public schools.

Conclusion: The MPCP voucher program does not violate the Establishment Clause of the First Amendment because (1) the purpose of the program is to provide low-income parents with an opportunity to have their children educated outside of the embattled Milwaukee Public School system; (2) it provides public aid to both sectarian and nonsectarian institutions on the basis of neutral, secular criteria that neither favor nor disfavor religion and only as a result of numerous private choices of the individual parents of school-age children; and (3) it is only subject to routine regulatory interaction. *See Jackson*, No. 97-0270 slip op. At *Id.* 26–52.

Notes

As we have seen, the first major case to deal with indirect aid to nonpublic schools was *Committee for Public Education v. Nyquist* (1973). In the facts of this case, the New York State legislature wanted to give grants to nonpublic schools that served a large number of low-income students. The money was given for the maintenance of school facilities. Additionally, low-income parents were given tuition reimbursements. Those parents who failed to qualify for the reimbursements were offered tax-deductions for their tuition costs. Basically, the state legislature saw that many families were suffering financial hardships in sending their children to private religious schools. If the state could create a law to give parents a choice in where they sent their children to school, the legislature felt that it could stop a potential decline in the attendance in nonpublic schools that could ultimately cause overcrowding in public schools.

The Supreme Court held that the New York State law was unconstitutional because it did not pass the Lemon Test. The law's purpose was to help religious schools. The Court found that most of the private schools attended were religiously affiliated, that those schools were pervasively sectarian in nature, and that the aid was not limited to secular use either by its nature or by its statutory restriction. The law was enacted to offer incentives to parents to send their children to private schools, most of which were religious. Thus, this was seen by the Court as indirect aid that had the intention of advancing religion and therefore, it violated the Establishment Clause of the First Amendment.

Nearly a decade later, the Supreme Court was presented with a similar state law to the one ruled on in **Nyquist**. This time, in *Mueller v. Allen*, the case concerned a tax deduction law in Minnesota. Under this law, taxpayers would be able to receive certain deductions for elementary and secondary school expenses. Parents could claim deductions if they spent money for allowable tuition, textbooks, and transportation expenses of their dependents. The benefit was available to parents of public as well as nonpublic school students, though evidence was introduced that only 79 of 815,000 public school students in the state had to pay tuition for public school.

As in **Nyquist**, taxpayers were receiving benefits if they sent their children to private schools. However, the Supreme Court ruled differently in this case. This time, by a slim 5-4 majority, the Supreme Court voted in favor of the Minnesota law. In the opinion of the Court, Justice Rehnquist showed why the law was able to pass Lemon Test muster. In his opinion, he specifically focused on the second prong of the Lemon Test, which deals with whether the law had the specific purpose of advancing a particular religion. Justice Rehnquist focused on the thinking of the Minnesota State legislature. Because the Minnesota law in question was a tax law, Rehnquist claimed that it "is presumed to be constitutional." Also, the fact that the deduction for textbooks, etc. in the statute also was part of a statutory scheme allowing deduction for other charitable donations/contributions suggested that the Minnesota legislature had a well thought-out plan to relieve taxpayers of various financial burdens. In this ruling, the Court is acknowledging that the intention of the law is to help *taxpayers*, whereas in the New York law in **Nyquist**, it directly helped nonpublic *schools*.

The court reached a similar conclusion in *Witters v. Washington Department of Services for the Blind* (1986). In this case, Witters, a blind student, applied to the Washington Commission for the Blind for vocational rehabilitation assistance. The Commission denied his request because Witters was planning to use the money for a Christian college he was attending, where he was planning on a religious vocation. When Witters took the cast to court, initially the lower courts ruled in favor of the Commission's decision stating that the aid would have the "primary affect of advancing religion."

However, the Supreme Court reversed the decision for similar reasons to **Mueller**. As in **Mueller**, the program in question did not have the intention of giving aid only to religious institutions. Also, the Supreme Court showed that there was no excessive entanglement. Assistance provided under the Washington program is paid directly to the student who then transmits it to the educational institution of his or her choice, so the program was found not to be skewed toward religion and it created no financial incentive for students who undertake sectarian education.

In 1990, the nations' first publicly funded voucher program was begun in the Milwaukee public school system. Amended in 1995, the voucher program provided state aid to low-income parents of students in the Milwaukee public school system. Again, as was the issue with cases dealing with indirect aid to religious institutions, the question is whether the voucher program in Milwaukee violated the First Amendment Establishment Clause.

In this case, *Jackson v. Benson*, the Supreme Court based its decision on whether the tuition voucher plan was able to pass the three prongs of the Lemon Test. First, there was a secular purpose, which was to allow low-income families an opportunity to send their children to different schools. Second, the law provided vouchers to these families on a neutral basis. It was up to the families to decide which school, secular or religious, to enroll their children. Finally, the government aid was given to parents to make their own private decision about how the money was to be used. Thus, there was no excessive entanglement between the government and the schools. Because it passed the three prongs of the Lemon Test, the Milwaukee voucher plan passed constitutional muster. However, this decision was applicable to the state of Wisconsin only.

This now brings us to the most recent cases dealing with tuition vouchers in the states of Ohio, Washington, and Florida. The constitutionality of a voucher program in Cleveland, Ohio, was found not to be in violation of the Establishment Clause. In *Zelman v. Simmons-Harris* (2002), Justice Rehnquist concluded that "previous case law in the Establishment Clause area such as **Mueller**, **Witters**, and **Benson** make it clear that where a government aid program is neutral with respect to religion, and provides assistance directly to a broad class of citizens who, in turn, direct government aid to religious schools wholly as a result of their own genuine and independent private choice, the program is not readily subject to challenge under the Establishment Clause." In effect, this decision of the Supreme Court has established tuition tax vouchers as being in accord with the First Amendment.

Index

About the Authors

Robert H. Palestini is Dean of Graduate and Continuing Education at Saint Joseph's University in Philadelphia. He has held the position of teacher, principal, superintendent, professor, and dean in his 40-plus years in education. His daughter, **Karen F. Palestini**, is a partner in the law firm of Reed, Smith, Shaw, and McClay and specializes in education law. She is also an adjunct professor at Saint Joseph's University.